Praise for the plays of Halley Feiffer

HOW TO MAKE FRIENDS AND THEN KILL THEM

"Ms. Feiffer . . . is building a reputation for fearlessness."

—Neil Genzlinger, *The New York Times*

"Thank God . . . for the warped creative mind of playwright/actress Halley Feiffer, who harnesses the weird to full, gory effect in *How to Make Friends and Then Kill Them,* an uproarious and deeply unsettling new dark comedy . . . Equally laugh-out-loud funny, jaw-droppingly gross, and thoroughly sad . . . Feiffer's unique, refreshing voice is one to which attention should be paid."

—David Gordon, *Theatermania*

"Disturbingly funny."

—Joe Dziemianowicz, *New York Daily News*

"A wicked comedy . . . Feiffer . . . is an expert comic actor with an appealingly skewed sensibility."

—Elisabeth Vincentelli, *New York Post*

"Feiffer . . . has a commendable eye for the absurd."

—*The New Yorker*

"There's great stuff here . . . dark and weird."

—Helen Snow, *Time Out New York*

I'M GONNA PRAY FOR YOU SO HARD

"Viciously funny . . . brutally effective. Feiffer takes a tough look at the forces that can bring us to our knees."

—Adam Feldman, *Time Out New York*

"A bone-chilling . . . punishing drama."

—Charles Isherwood, *The New York Times*

"Blistering, blackly funny."
        —Joe Dziemianowicz, *New York Daily News*

"One minute you're laughing, the next you're cringing . . . the play sticks in your head like a crazy nightmare."
        —Elisabeth Vincentelli, *New York Post*

"Funny, scary, and completely over the top in its own right . . . goes straight for the jugular through the heart."
        —Robert Hofler, *The Wrap*

"Provocative, sensitive, shocking and often very unsettling . . . polished and probing. One of the best plays I've seen this season."
        —Rex Reed, *New York Observer*

"Exhilaratingly toxic."   —Joe McGovern, *Entertainment Weekly*

"A hard-hearted stunner." —Michael Schulman, *The New Yorker*

"Halley Feiffer's ferocious, explosive dialogue in *I'm Gonna Pray For You So Hard* is in a class of its own."
        —Lee Kinney, *TheEasy.com*

"It's a fearless piece of work, riveting and hilarious."
        —Robert Feldberg, *Bergen Record*

Photo: Ahron Foster

HALLEY FEIFFER is a New York-based writer and actress. Her full-length plays include *I'm Gonna Pray For You So Hard* (World Premiere Atlantic Theater Company, 2015), *How To Make Friends And Then Kill Them* (World Premiere Rattlestick Playwrights Theater, 2014), and *A Funny Thing Happened On The Way To The Gynecologic Oncology Unit At Memorial Sloan Kettering Cancer Center of New York City* (World Premiere MCC Theater, 2016). Her plays have been developed by Manhattan Theatre Club, Second Stage, New York Theater Workshop, LAByrinth Theater Company, The O'Neill, and elsewhere. Her work has been commissioned by Manhattan Theatre Club, The Alfred P. Sloan Foundation, Williamstown Theater Festival and Playwrights Horizons. She won a Theater World Award for her performance in the 2011 Broadway revival of *The House of Blue Leaves*, and co-wrote and starred in the 2013 film *He's Way More Famous Than You.* She is a writer on the Starz series *The One Percent.*

HOW TO MAKE FRIENDS AND THEN KILL THEM

A PLAY BY
HALLEY FEIFFER

OVERLOOK DUCKWORTH
New York · London

CAUTION: Professionals and amateurs are hereby warned that performance of the Play HOW TO MAKE FRIENDS AND THEN KILL THEM is subject to payment of a royalty. The Play is fully protected under the copyright laws of the United States of America, and of all countries covered by the International Copyright Union (including the Dominion of Canada and the rest of the British Commonwealth), and of all countries covered by the Pan-American Copyright Convention, the Universal Copyright Convention, the Berne Convention, and of all countries with which the United States has reciprocal copyright relations. All rights, including without limitation professional/ amateur stage rights, motion picture, recitation, lecturing, public reading, radio broadcasting, television, video or sound recording. all other forms of mechanical, electronic and digital reproduction, transmission and distribution, such as CD, DVD, the Internet, private and file-sharing networks, information storage and retrieval systems, photocopying, and the rights of translation into foreign languages are strictly reserved. Particular emphasis is placed upon the matter of readings, permission for which must be secured from the Author's agent in writing. Inquiries concerning rights should be addressed to ICM Partners 730 Fifth Avenue New York, NY 10019. Attn: Di Glazer.

This edition first published in the United States and the United Kingdom in 2016 by Overlook Duckworth, Peter Mayer Publishers, Inc.

NEW YORK
141 Wooster Street
New York, NY 10012
www.overlookpress.com
For bulk and special sales, please contact sales@overlookny.com,
or write us at above address.

LONDON
30 Calvin Street
London E1 6NW
info@duckworth-publishers.co.uk
www.ducknet.co.uk
For bulk and special sales, please contact sales@duckworth-publishers.co.uk,
or write us at the above address.

Copyright © 2016 by Halley Feiffer

All rights reserved. No part of this publication may be reproduced or transmitted in any form or by any means, electronic or mechanical, including photocopy, recording, or any information storage and retrieval system now known or to be invented, without permission in writing from the publisher, except by a reviewer who wishes to quote brief passages in connection with a review written for inclusion in a magazine, newspaper, or broadcast.

Cataloging-in-Publication Data is available from the Library of Congress
A catalogue record for this book is available from the British Library

Book design and type formatting by Bernard Schleifer
Manufactured in the United States of America
ISBN 978-1-4683-1252-2 (US)
ISBN 978-0-7156-5144-5 (UK)
1 3 5 7 9 10 8 6 4 2

HOW TO
MAKE
FRIENDS
AND THEN
KILL THEM

PREFACE

In the course of the fifteen scenes of *How To Make Friends and Then Kill Them*, Halley Feiffer tracks two sisters and a friend through their obsessive loves, hatreds, rivalries, fears, cruelties, successes, failures, small choices becoming defining points for life over a nineteen-year period, starting at age 10 when the taste of gin is the smell of an adult, ending at age 29 in destruction [the age Feiffer was when she wrote it]. They act out their roles of what they think it means to be an adult, to be a woman in power.

It takes place for the most part in a room with two ways out—one leading to the world, one down to the cellar. That route is only taken once. The walls are lined with shelves of every kind of alcoholic drink.

I asked the playwright to tell me the story of her play.

"Three damaged women use each other to fill each other's emotional holes, progressively fail to do so and, in so doing, warp each other's lives beyond repair."

When I read this play, I thought two things. Jean Genet and Alicia Silverstone. Yes. That terrific movie *Clueless*, which used Jane Austen's *Emma* as a giddy leaping off point.

Are Feiffer's two sisters descendants of Genet's Claire and Solange? [Devoid of Genet's political and psycho-sexual implications and that's a whole lot of devoid but let me go on. I'm trying to get a handle on this play.] Did Halley Feiffer pull the *Clueless* tactic on Genet? I asked Halley if she had read *The Maids*.

"I didn't read it until after I'd finished my play. I read *The Maids* and said, I have been here before. As if Genet's sensibility had been waiting. I read the play thinking it was one thing, and then the bottom would fall out and the play would become something else, again and again. I loved its constant shift, but even more the sadistic and cruel way the maids treated each other, the way women often do, and how early it starts."

Feiffer gives the children a very specific voice.

Where had I heard it before?

Yes. Those raging female indie rock groups who blasted out of the Pacific Northwest in the 1990s with Patti Smith as their muse. Girl bands like Sleater-Kinney, whose lead singer Corin Tucker's first recording was a rage about her period.

I asked Feiffer if she knew Sleater-Kinney. She said "I can't believe out of all the bands on earth you picked up on Sleater-Kinney. You're this [I heard her searching for the word—old? white-haired? She settled on . . .] long time playwright. How do you know Sleater-Kinney?"

Sorry, Halley. This is about you.

"I first heard them in 2006 when I was acting in Eric Bogosian's *Suburbia* at Second Stage. Kieran Culkin seduced my character with a Sleater-Kinney song called either *Jumper* or *Jumpers*. I liked this song because either way it sounded like suicide and it was coming out of women's mouths. The show's sound designer named Muttt with three t's put together a bunch of female punk rock songs for me and it opened up a world. A new voice of feminism. I really wasn't much into music before that. I never listened to the words but made up my own words to the music and the title. I started listening. You know Sleater-Kinney? I'm really impressed." [NOTE: Ms Feiffer only said it once. The compliment so pleased me I put it in twice.]

How do you define feminism? What does that mean today?

"To me being a feminist means what it's always meant. No more than wanting the same rights as men. Feminism is the freedom for women to behave as repugnantly as men—if we don't get the help we need. The guys in *True West* treat each other abominably. Nobody calls Sam Shepard misogynistic. People have called me sexist, do I hate women? Men do it all the time but women aren't supposed to. I've treated people this way and, yes, have been treated this way. Why did I write it? Perhaps to break the chain."

Is the three-character play autobiographical?

"I was an only child until I was ten. My play is more the fantasy of an only child. It started out as a group of short plays called *It's Just Weird Now: Short Plays About Friendship* about female friendships, women treating each other horribly. Someone asked me to find a narrative link for those plays. Instead I wrote this play."

Influences?

"The first play I ever saw was *Guys and Dolls* with Nathan Lane and I loved the dazzle of it, but the first play that had a profound energizing effect on me was Arthur Kopit's *Oh Dad, Poor Dad, Mamma's Hung You In the Closet and I'm Feelin' So Sad*. I read that and didn't know the stage was a place where you could have a talking fish. I wanted to be there."

She is there. It's called now. Halley Feiffer is 30. Her last play *I'm Gonna Pray For You Hard* staked out emotional terrain she'll be exploring the rest of her life. There's this play you hold in your hands right now. Her next is called *A Funny Thing Happened On The Way To the Gynecologic Oncology Unit at Memorial Sloan Kettering Cancer Center of New York City.*

I can't wait.

—John Guare
  July 10, 2015

ACKNOWLEDGMENTS

A major THANK YOU to the generous people and institutions whose contribution was crucial in the creation of this play:

Jenny Allen, Jules Feiffer, Lina Makdisi, Maya Kazan, Darren Katz, Chris Burney, Brooke Bloom, Jenni Barber, Greta Lee, Ari Edelson, Reiko Aylesworth, Mandy Siegfried, Greg Keller, Kate Maguire, Phillip Witte, Sarah Kauffman, Caitlin Teeley, Samantha Richert, John Eisner, Desiree Akhavan, Jesse Eisenberg, Evan Cabnet, Betty Gilpin, Alison Pill, Cristin Milioti, Tracee Chimo, Sarah Steele, Nikhil Melnechuk, Bob Holman, Robyn Goodman, Josh Fiedler, Jill Rafson, Daryl Roth, Joshua Astrachan, John Guare, David Van Asselt, Daniel Talbott, Brian Miskell, Brian Long, Jessica Amato, Shira-Lee Shalit, Lillith Fallon, Belle Caplis, Stephanie Seward, Wesleyan University, and The Rattlestick Playwrights Theatre. Second Stage Theatre, The Drama Bookshop, The LARK, Berkshire Theatre Group, The Bowery Poetry Club, LAByrinth Theater Company, Daniel Kluger, Andromache Chalfant, Jessica Pabst, Tyler Micoleau, Amanda Perry, Mikey Denis, Eugenia Furneaux, Katya Campbell, Keira Keeley, Jen Ponton, Elizabeth Carlson, Kip Fagan and Di Glazer.

This play was developed with generous support from The Orchard Project, SPACE on Ryder Farm and the Cape Cod Theatre Project.

CAST OF CHARACTERS

The world premiere of *How to Make Friends and Then Kill Them* was produced by Rattlestick Playwrights Theatre, New York City, 2013. Directed by Kip Fagan.

ADA	Katya Campbell
SAM	Keira Keeley
DORRIE	Jen Ponton

CHARACTERS

ADA: Ages 10–29; played by one actress. Beautiful, charismatic, alcoholic. Wants to be an actress but her obsession with alcohol holds her back.

SAM: Ages 9–28; played by one actress. Ada's sister. Less beautiful than Ada; plucky, strong-willed, whip-smart. Wants to be a graphic novelist but her obsession with her sister holds her back.

DORRIE: Ages 10–29; played by one actress. Insecure, hugely self-conscious, desperate to give and receive love. Possessed of one of the purest hearts there is. Her sole purpose is her devotion to Ada and Sam.

SETTING

Present Day. A suburban American town not far from New York City.

PRODUCTION NOTES

The set should be spare and minimal. All design elements should have a neglected quality.

Ellipses in the text indicate a character having a thought—they do not necessarily need to translate into significant pauses.

SCENE 1

Darkness.

<u>*The voices of three girls scream:*</u> ***"CHILDHOOD!!!"***

> *We hear Randy Newman's cheerful and heartwarming song "You've Got a Friend In Me" playing, and then . . .*

> *. . . the sound of hands slapping against each other.*

> *Lights creep up on* ADA *and* SAM *— ten and nine years old — in their kitchen. They wear matching school uniforms.* ADA*'s skirt is rolled up higher than* SAM*'s.* ADA *wears a string of beads around her neck.* SAM *has a pencil tucked behind her ear.*

> *They play a hand game — very intensely, and very rapidly. They play it as if their lives depended on it.*

> *We see that the music is playing from a transistor radio, on the kitchen counter.*

> *The room has two doors — one leading off to the rest of the house, and one down to the cellar. The back wall of the kitchen is lined with shelves, which are filled with bottles of seemingly every kind of alcohol.*

> *Laying out on the kitchen table is a sketchbook and a pencil.*

> *After several rounds of the hand game,* SAM *messes up, and the game falls apart.*

ADA

You messed up, that was six.

SAM

I'm sorry, I thought it was five.

ADA

Yeah, I could see you did.
> *Beat.*

SAM

Do you want to play again . . .?

ADA

No. I don't.

Beat. Then—

ADA *uses a chair to get up and stand on the table.*

ADA

Can you turn off the radio and get the flashlight? I would like to prac-tice my mon-o-logue.

SAM *nods, scurries over to the radio; turns it off. She opens a cupboard and removes a large, unwieldy flash-light. Scurries back over to the table and squats down, shining the flashlight up onto* ADA, *as if it were a footlight on a stage.*

ADA

Okay, say: ". . . and . . . Action!"

SAM

. . .and . . . Action!

ADA *suddenly strikes a pose—twists her body into some sort of highly unnatural, dramatic position.*

ADA
(Performatively.)

I just . . . can't help . . . but think . . . I am . . . ex*tremely* . . . beautiful.

A beat. She changes her "blocking": strikes a sort of sexy pose.

ADA

Sometimes . . .? While brushing my teeth? Or picking a blackhead?? Out of my nose??? I'll step back, and look at my face in the mirror, and I'll see . . . me . . .!

(She strikes a sort of modern dance-y pose.)

And I'm always . . . so pleasantly . . . *surprised* . . .!

(She strikes a sort of heroin-chic pose.)

Because I'm . . . *gorgeous*.

She holds her absurd pose.

A beat. Then—

SAM
(Applauding.)
Yaaaay . . .!

ADA
(Hopping off the table.)
What did you think of the changes?

SAM
They're really strong.

ADA
I'm still working on it.

> ADA *hops of the table.* SAM *turns off the flashlight, and looks at* ADA, *admiringly.*

SAM
Can I draw you for a second?

ADA
Fine. But just for a second. I find posing for your drawings very boring.

> SAM *beams, grabs her sketchbook off the table and her pencil from behind her ear, and hunkers down.*

> ADA *strikes a brand new dramatic pose.* SAM *begins to sketch her.*

SAM
(Sketching with incredible seriousness.)
You've always been so pretty, Ada.

ADA
I hate it when you tell me that, Sam.

SAM
I know, I know—I didn't forget. I just like telling you.

ADA
But I hate it *soooooo* much.

SAM
I know.
(Beat.)
But do you really?

> *Beat.* ADA *considers. . . .*

ADA

Sometimes I like it.

SAM

I thought so . . .!

ADA

I mean I like it when *other* people do it.

SAM

Oh.

ADA

But I don't really like it when *you* do it.

SAM

Yeah.

ADA

There's something really creepy about the way you say "soooooo pretty."

SAM

Uh-huh. . . .

ADA

It's like you're a Frenchman trying to seduce me, or something.

SAM

(Mortified.)

Totally. Yeah.

SAM*'s eyes start to well up. She rubs her eyes, vigorously.*

ADA

Are you okay?

SAM

My contact lenses are clouding up.

ADA

I told Mom you were too young to get contacts.

SAM

I'm just a year younger than you.

ADA

But mine are purely cosmetic.

ADA *begins practicing ballet moves.*

ADA

(Doing a relevé.)

I like to fantasize about how one day? I'm not gonna have to be here, posing for your gay drawings.

SAM

(Rubbing her eyes.)

Huh.

ADA

(Doing a plié.)

I'm gonna be off at *college*, riding a *bike* and eating in the *dining* hall and having sex with my prof*essors*, et cetera.

SAM

(Snorts.)

You're gonna be a slut.

ADA

(Doing an arabesque; with great pride.)

Mm-hmmmmmmm!

> ADA *quits dancing, grabs a chair from the kitchen table and pushes it over to the shelves on the back wall; she stands on the chair, and examines the bottles of alcohol.*
>
> SAM *continues to sketch her.*
>
> ADA *takes a shining blue bottle of gin off a shelf, and turns it around in her hands, admiring it.*
>
> *She screws the top off the gin bottle and smells it.*

SAM

What are you doing . . .?

ADA

I like the way it smells.

SAM

I think it smells terrible.

ADA

I think it smells like being an adult.

> *She screws the top back on the gin bottle and places it back on the shelf.*

SAM

(Still sketching ADA.)

Hold still. . . .

ADA

Euuugh, stop *drawing* me—I can feel your beady little eyes boring a
hole into my psychic *en-er-gy.*

> SAM *puts down her sketchbook and pen, rubs her eyes.*

SAM

Fine.

ADA

(Turning to SAM.)
Will you bruise me so Mom will pay more attention to me?

SAM

Where do you want me to bruise you?

ADA

(Rolling up the sleeve of her shirt.)
Here. On my arm.

SAM

How???

ADA

Just wrap your fingers around it and squeeze, really really tight.

SAM

(Nervous.)
Okay. . . .

> SAM *sticks the pencil behind her ear, wraps her fingers
> around* ADA*'s arm and squeezes, really tight.*

ADA

Ooh. Thank you.

SAM

(Squeezing ADA*'s arm as hard as she can.)*
Is this good . . .?

ADA

(Wincing a bit at the pain.)
Yes. Please stop asking me to val-i-date you.

SAM

Sorry.

> SAM *squeezes harder.*

ADA

Ow! That's good. Stop.

SAM *releases her grip on* ADA*'s arm. They look at it.*

SAM

You think that'll bruise?

ADA

I hope so.

(*Beat.*)

Can you open the cellar door? For some vent-il-ation?

SAM

That doesn't make any sense.

ADA

Just *do* it. It's hot in here.

SAM

Fine.

SAM *opens the cellar door. It opens onto a dark, long, spooky-looking staircase.*

ADA

Ahhhh. That's better.

SAM

(*Shudders.*)

Uggggh. I hate that spooky staircase.

SAM *sits back down, removes her pencil from behind her ear and starts drawing something from her imagination.*

ADA

What are you doing.

SAM

(*Distracted.*)

. . . what . . .?

ADA

WHAT ARE YOU DOING???

SAM

Oh! I'm . . . drawing . . .?

ADA

What are you drawing.

SAM

Something . . . from my imagination . . .?

ADA

Well stop.

> SAM

Why?

> ADA

'Cause I'm bored!

> SAM

Ada. . . .

> ADA
>
> *(Matter-of-factly.)*

You can't *draw* stuff from your imagin*ation*, anyway. You can only draw stuff that's in *front* of you. If you draw stuff from your imagination, it always looks fake, and dumb. And fake.

> SAM

P.F. Touchane draws stuff *only* from his imagination. He's the best artist in the world.

> ADA

I don't even know who that is.

> *Beat.*

> ADA

Will you let me brush your hair?

> SAM

Fine.

> SAM *stops drawing.* ADA *opens up a drawer and removes a hairbrush. She moves behind* SAM *and starts to brush her hair.*

> SAM
>
> *(Sniffs the air.)*

It smells like cigarettes in here. . . .

> ADA
>
> *(Matter-of-factly.)*

I was smoking.

> SAM

WHAT?!?

> ADA
>
> *(With a nonchalant shrug.)*

I tried it.

> SAM

WHEN ?!?!?

> ADA

When you were at softball practice.
> *(Beat)*

SAM

(Softly.)

Oh.

ADA

What.

SAM

(Softly.)

I just—I can't believe you did that . . . without telling me. . . .

ADA *shrugs; keeps brushing.*

A beat. Then—

ADA

Also I got my period.

SAM

<u>*WHAT ?!?!?!?!?!?!*</u>

ADA

Just kidding.

SAM

I hate you.

ADA *stops brushing* SAM*'s hair. She puts the hairbrush down, pats* SAM*'s freshly-brushed hair.*

A beat. Then—

ADA

It's never weird with us, is it?

SAM

What do you mean.

ADA

I mean like when there are weird moments? Between friends?? When it gets . . .

(Searches for the word.)

. . . *awk*-ward . . .??? I hate that.

SAM

Me too.

ADA

But with us, that never happens.

SAM

Yeah.

Beat.

ADA

It wasn't that fun, smoking the cigarette, anyway.

SAM

Where did you get it?

ADA

From Mom.

SAM

She gave it to you?!?

ADA

No, you idiot—I stole it.

SAM

I never see Mom smoking.

ADA

She smokes when she goes out to bars.

SAM

(Snorts.)
So like, every night.

Beat.

ADA

That wasn't very nice.

SAM

Sorry.

A beat. ADA *examines her cuticles.*

ADA

I smell them on her when she comes back.

SAM

I'm always asleep when she comes back.

ADA

That's 'cause you don't care about her as much as I do. I'm always careful to sleep lightly when she goes out, so that I can make sure she's all right when she comes back. Last night she left the car running in the driveway with all the lights on and everything, and when I went down to see why the engine was still on, Mommy was still in the car, behind the wheel, asleep with her mouth open. I guess she fell asleep while she was getting out of the car or something. I picked her up and helped her up the stairs and into bed. I help everyone. I'm always so nice.

(Beat; she thinks about how nice she is; sighs.)

I could smell the cigarettes on her really strongly. This morning I asked her why she fell asleep in the car and she yelled at me. She told me not to judge her, and that she deserves to have fun like everyone else . . . .

>   *(Beat; considers . . .)*

. . . which I guess makes sense.

>   *Beat.*

>   SAM

I heard her yelling at you.

>   ADA

I know. I don't know why she always yells at me and not at you. I don't know why you never come to help me when she's yelling at me.

>   *(Beat.)*

I was mad that she yelled at me so I snooped in her bag while she was pooping and I found the cigarettes. She smokes *Newport Ultra Lights*.

>   SAM

How do you know? How do you know all this stuff I don't???

>   ADA

I don't know, maybe I'm more observant.

>   SAM

I'm observant. You used to say I'd make a good detective.

>   ADA

Well you're not observant any*more*. You always have your *head* up your ass now, with your homework, with your dumb *comic strips*.

>   SAM

They're called *graphic novellas*.

>   ADA
>   *(Suddenly jumping down her throat.)*

HEY. I'm not *stupid*, Sam! Just because I'm really pretty and I don't *love* getting all A's and drawing stupid *comics* like you doesn't mean I'm like a dumb *idiot*.

>   SAM
>   *(Rubbing her eyes.)*

I never . . . *said* that . . .!

>   ADA
>   *(With a sudden fiery intensity.)*

I write *mon-o-logues* and I *practice* them and *edit* them and practice them *again*. And *you* seem to think it's all a *joke—yooooou* just can't wait to get back to your gay little *drawings*. But you're gonna be sorry. Do you know why?

 (Getting up in SAM*'s face.)*

<u>Do. You. Know. Why?</u>

 SAM *shakes her head, meekly.*

SAM

N-no. . .

ADA

Because I'm gonna grow up to be a *huge* success! A giant movie star, on the silver screen—ten feet wide, twenty feet high! And the whole world will *parade my funeral* in Times Square!!!

 A beat. SAM *rubs her eyes.*

SAM

Okay. I'm sorry. I know you take . . . acting . . . seriously. . . .

ADA

It's a <u>craft</u>.

SAM

I know. I'm *sorry*. I didn't mean to . . . belittle it. . . .

 Beat.

ADA

What's "belittle" mean?

SAM

 (Sweetly.)

It doesn't matter.

 SAM *reaches her arms toward* ADA, *trying to hug her.* ADA
 brushes her away.

ADA

Euuugh, don't hug me. You're all sweaty on account of beginning puberty.

SAM

 (Baffled.)

No, I'm not. . . .

ADA

 (Turning away from her; casually.)

Often we can't sense these things in ourselves.

 Devastated, SAM *smells under her armpits.*

 ADA *begins practicing ballet moves again.*

 A beat. Then—

SAM

I'm gonna go change. Then can we hug?

ADA

(Doing a relevé.)

Why do you care so much about *hugging*? That's so gay.

SAM

I don't like it when we fight. I like to . . . create closure . . . with a *hug*. . . .

ADA

(Doing a plie.)

This isn't a fight.

SAM

Well . . . when it's *weird*, then. . . .

ADA

(Doing an arabesque; aggressive.)

It's not *weird*—it's never *weird* with us, remember???

SAM

You're right, you're right—it's never weird.

ADA *turns away from* SAM, *continues practicing ballet moves.*

SAM *watches her, enraptured.*

A beat. Then—

SAM

I'm sorry, Ada.

ADA

(Dancing; sing-song.)

Okaaayyy. . . .

SAM

I love you Ada.

ADA

(Dancing; absently, sing-song.)

I kno-o-o-owww. . . .

SAM

I . . .

(Her voice cracking, ever so slightly.)

I . . . *need* you . . . Ada . . ..

ADA *ignores her, sings to herself as she dances.*

ADA

(Singing to herself.)
I just . . . can't help . . .

SAM

. . . Ada . . .?

ADA

(Ignoring SAM*; singing to herself.)*
. . . but think . . . I am . . .

SAM

Ada? Say you—*need me*, too. . . .

ADA

(Continuing to ignore SAM*; dancing and singing to herself.)*
. . . extreeeeeeeeemely . . . beeeeautifuuuul . . .!

SAM *looks at* ADA, *rubs her eyes; then—she runs off.*

*Oblivious—in her own world—*ADA *continues to dance. She pirouettes, fiercely. One, two, three.*

Then—she looks at her arm.

SAM

(Calling off to SAM*; gleeful.)*
It's bruising!!!

SCENE 2

ADA and DORRIE make cutout snowflakes in their class-room, as ten-year-olds. They both wear the same school uniform. ADA has a new string of beads around her neck.

DORRIE is sweet-looking but has terrible, terrible acne all over her face and body. She also moves with a slight, almost undetectable limp.

ADA

What's wrong with your face.

DORRIE

What?

ADA

WHAT'S WRONG WITH YOUR FACE???

DORRIE

Oh. Um. I have "childhood acne."

ADA

What's that.

DORRIE

It means—it means I have "pathological precocious puberty" which is "the early onset of puberty caused by an underlying medical condition" which in my case is an endocrine disorder.

ADA

What's an endocrine disorder.

DORRIE

It means my glands excrete sex hormones too early.

ADA

Hahahaha!

DORRIE

It's not funny.

ADA

I'll laugh at what I want to!

DORRIE

Sorry.

ADA

Also it is funny.

DORRIE

Okay.

    (Beat.)

ADA

Why do you walk with a limp.

DORRIE

I don't.

ADA

Yeah you do.

DORRIE

Shoot. You noticed that?

ADA

Yuppers.

DORRIE

Shoot. I thought I was hiding it. I have early-onset fibromyalgia. I guess I have a lot of problems.

ADA

What other problems do you have.

DORRIE

Just, others.

ADA

Like what? I find problems int-er-est-ing.

DORRIE

Oh, just irritable bowel syndrome (I had to have a colonoscopy even though I'm only ten, it was sad), and I have insomnia—sometimes I lie in bed all night just waiting to fall asleep and then it never happens and then I just get out of bed and go to school in the morning as if everything is normal except I didn't sleep at all the night before, it's scary, and then sometimes I fall asleep *in class* the next day, it's so embarrassing, and the teacher gets mad at me, she's like, "DORRIE! DON'T FALL ASLEEP IN CLASS!" because she thinks I'm falling asleep because I'm bored but I'm *not*—I have a *medical condition!* Also I have a fair amount of psychiatric problems? Like I take Cymbalta, Buspirone and Geodon for depression-slash-anxiety, also I have very mild ADHD I guess but the doctor says I don't need to take medication for that but I wish I did because I like taking medication, also I pick all the skin off my thumbs because of my anxiety so I have barely any skin on my thumbs wanna see no never mind my mom said I should stop showing people, also I've had fourteen teeth pulled, I had two rows of teeth at one point— when I ate mashed potatoes I had to spit them out 'cause they were so bloody because my mouth was so bloody, and that's it I guess those are all my problems.

    (She smiles, queasily.)

ADA

So that's why no one talks to you, huh?

DORRIE

I guess.

    Beat.

ADA

What's your name?

DORRIE

Dorrie.

ADA

I like that name.

DORRIE

Thanks.

ADA

I'm Ada.

DORRIE

I know.

ADA

No one talks to me either.

DORRIE

I know.

ADA

    (Suddenly defensive.)

What do you mean?!

DORRIE

I just—I see you, with your sister, all the time. Your twin?

ADA

She's not my twin—she's a year younger.

DORRIE

Oh.

ADA

Our mom had sex twice, like nine months apart.

DORRIE

Okay.

ADA

Just kidding. I don't know. She's in our grade, though. She skipped a grade. I fucking hate how smart she is, sometimes.

DORRIE

She looks nice.

ADA

She's an asshole. There's something wrong with her.

DORRIE

Really?

ADA

Idunno.

> *A beat.*

> *They continue making their cutout snowflakes.*

ADA

Why do we have to make these gay-ass snowflakes anyway?

DORRIE

For the winter dance.

ADA

I wish this was a Halloween dance.

DORRIE

Me too.

ADA

You're just saying that 'cause I said it.

DORRIE

Yeah.

> *Beat.*

ADA

What's your name?

DORRIE

I just told you.

ADA

I forgot already. You're not very memorable.

DORRIE

Oh. It's Dorrie.

ADA

I remembered that time.

DORRIE

Sorry.

> *Beat.*

ADA

I could be popular, you know. If I didn't have my sister, holding me back.

DORRIE

Yeah, you could, definitely, I bet.

ADA

Let's hang out sometime.

DORRIE

Okay!

> *A beat;* ADA *studies* DORRIE.

ADA

What's your name again?

DORRIE

Dorrie.

ADA

Dorrie.

DORRIE

Thanks.

SCENE 3

The sisters' kitchen, empty. The phone rings.

Sound of the girls clumping quickly down the stairs. Then —both girls come running in, sprinting toward the phone.

ADA

(Running to the phone.)

I'll get it! It's probably for me.

She picks up the phone. SAM *pants, stands near her; listens.*

ADA

(Into phone.)

Hello?

(Beat.)

Oh hey!

(Beat.)

Haha f. . . .

(Beat.)

Hahaha you're funny, haha. . . .

SAM *mouths "Who is it?"*

ADA *ignores her.*

ADA

(Into phone.)

That's so sweet! Oh my gosh, you're *soooooo* sweet.

SAM *mouths "Who is it?" again.*

ADA *ignores her.*

ADA

No you! No you. No you you you you you you YOU HAHAHAHAHA!

SAM *mouths "Who is it?" again, a bit more frantically.*

ADA

(Into phone:)

Hold on one second?

(To SAM*:)*

It's Dorrie.

(Into phone:)

Hi, what were you saying . . .?

(Beat.)

Hey can I give you a call later? And let you know???

(Beat.)

Okay. . . .

(Beat; laughs.)

Okay . . .!

(Beat; laughs; in a funny voice:)

HO-O-O-O-KAAAAY!

ADA *laughs.*

SAM *laughs too, at* ADA*'s funny voice.*

ADA *looks sternly at* SAM.

A beat. Then—

ADA

(Into phone:)

Okayloveyoubye.

ADA *hangs up.*

A beat.

Then—

SAM

That was Dorrie?

ADA

Yeah.

SAM

Cool.

ADA

What?

SAM

What? Nothing.

ADA

You seem weird now.

SAM

(A bit defensive.)

Okay. . . .

ADA

What???

SAM

I'm not.

ADA

Okay.

SAM

Okay.
>   *(Beat.)*
Good.
>   *Beat.*

ADA

You do seem weird, though.

SAM

Well, I don't feel weird.

ADA

Okay. . . .
>   *(Beat.)*
But I'm saying you *seem* weird to me, and you can't really deny that.

SAM

Well. . . . I guess I can't "*deny*" the way I *seem* to you but—

ADA

Right, you can't.

SAM

Right, I know, I just *said* that.

ADA

Okay.

SAM

Okay.

>   *A beat.*
>   SAM *smiles, widely, at* ADA, *to show she is not feeling weird.*
>   ADA *smiles back, mockingly, at* SAM.

SAM

What?!?

ADA

See?!? Something's weird!

                              SAM
No it's not, it's just weird *now* since you said I seemed weird.

                              ADA
Right, but if you *seem* weird to me, then something *is* weird, is what I'm
saying.

     (Beat.)
And it makes *me* feel weird.

     (Beat.)
Because if there are two people and one of them feels weird then the
other person is going to, too.

     (Beat.)
I mean like I can't control how I'm feeling—I just feel.

          Beat. SAM *is silent.*

                              ADA
Okay. . . . Well, maybe I can't tell how you're feeling. . . .

                              SAM
     (Very defensive.)
No, you *can't.*

                              ADA
I *know* I can't, Sam, that's why I just *said* that.

                              SAM
What?! Why are you *being* like that?!?

                              ADA
Like *what?!?*

                              SAM
Nothing.

          Beat.

                              ADA
Were you going to say . . . "weird"?

                              SAM
No.

          Beat.

                              ADA
     (With mischievous humor.)
I think you we-e-e-e-ere. . . .

                              SAM
     (With a little smile.)
No. . . .

ADA

(Playful; sing-song.)

I think you were . . . were were were were *were* . . .!

> *As* ADA *sings this improvised song, she creeps her fingers up* SAM*'s arm, like a little spider, sort of tickling her.*
>
> *Suddenly,* SAM *swats* ADA*'s hand away—almost violently.*

SAM

No, I *wasn't!* I was gonna say—I don't *know* what I was gonna say, that's why I didn't *say* it.

ADA

(Stunned by SAM*'s outburst.)*

Okay.

> ADA *looks away.*
>
> SAM*'s eyes stay on* ADA*, for a moment; then—she looks away, too.*
>
> *A long, long moment of the two of them not doing any-thing, just looking away from each other.*
>
> SAM *begins to twist the tip of her sock around her wrist, anxiously.*
>
> *When the silence is almost excruciating—*
>
> SAM *coughs.*

ADA

(Without looking at her.)

Bless you.

> *Beat.*

SAM

(Not looking at her.)

That was a cough. You don't need to say "*bless you*" for a cough.

> *Beat.*

ADA

I'm going to open the cellar door. For some ventilation.

SAM

I don't care.

> ADA *gets up and opens the cellar door. Then, she sits back down.*
>
> *They go back to sitting and not looking at each other.*

SAM *pulls her twisted-up sock off her foot, and ties it around her wrist. She suddenly laughs to herself.*

> SAM
> *(Softly.)*

. . . hahahaha. . . .

> ADA
> *(Without looking at* SAM*; softly.)*

What are you laughing at.

> SAM

Nothing.

> *(Beat.)*

I made a sock-bracelet.

> (ADA *turns and looks.)*

I thought it was funny.

> *Beat.*

> ADA

It is.

> SAM

Oh. Good.

> *A beat. Then–*

ADA *reaches down and pulls her sock off her foot. She tries to tie it around her wrist, but it is too short.*

> ADA

My sock is too short.

> SAM

Here.

> SAM *takes her other sock off her other foot and ties it onto* ADA*'s wrist.*

> ADA
> *(Smiles.)*

Thanks.

> SAM
> *(Admires her sock-bracelet.)*

Now we're sock-bracelet sisters.

> ADA

Yaaaaay. Sock-bracelet sisters.

> *They make their sock-bracelets play with each other and kiss each other, etc.*

ADA & SAM
(Together; improvising a song.)
*Sock-bracelet sisters, la la la la la la, singing in the la la, loodie doodie
doo doo. . . .*

> *They crack each other up with their made-up lyrics.*

ADA & SAM
Hahahahaha!

> *They make their sock-bracelets high-five each other.*

ADA & SAM
(High-fiving each other's arms with their sock-bracelets.)
Yeah!

> *They laugh.*

ADA & SAM
Hahahahaha!!!

> *Then—*ADA *swats* SAM *in the face with her sock-bracelet
> arm, playfully.*

ADA
(Playfully swatting.)
Bam!

SAM
Ohh!

> *They laugh.*

ADA & SAM
Hahahahaha!!!

> *Then—*SAM *shoves* ADA, *backwards, playfully.*

SAM
(Playfully shoving.)
BOOM!!

ADA
OOOH!!

> *They laugh.*

ADA & SAM
HAHAHAHAHAHAHAHA!!!

> *Then—*ADA *pushes* SAM, *hard, backwards, playfully.*

ADA
(Playfully pushing.)
SHAZZZAAAMMMMMMMMMM!!!!!!

SAM

(Falling on her butt.)

AAAAAAAIIIIIIIIIEEE!!!!!!

They laugh and laugh and laugh.

ADA & SAM

HAHAHAHAHAHAHAHAHAHAHAHAHAHAHAHAHAHAHAHAHAHA!!!!!!

When the laughter dies down . . .

They let out a simultaneous, satisfied sigh.

ADA & SAM

(A simultaneous sigh.)

Huuuuuuuuuuuuhhhhhhhhhh . . ..

Beat. Then—

ADA

(Helping SAM *up.)*

I'm glad it's not weird anymore.

SAM

Me too.

(Beat.)

ADA

So you're saying you *did* think it was weird before. . . .

SAM

Oh my *god* Ada—

ADA

But you just—

SAM

Oh my *god!*

ADA

But you said—

> SAM *suddenly lunges toward* ADA *and claps her hand over* ADA*'s mouth. It is an action that is playful, but also serious.*

SAM

Will you *stop?*

ADA *nods.*

SAM

Will you???

ADA *nods.*

SAM

I mean it. I know I'm smiling right now because you're annoying me in
a funny way, but sometimes it's not in a funny way, and I do really need
you to stop, I'm serious.

>ADA *nods.*

SAM

Okay.

>*(Beat.)*

Good.

>SAM *slowly removes her hand from* ADA*'s mouth, keeping
>her eyes glued on* ADA. ADA *is being silent, behaving herself.*

>*Then—*

>ADA *suddenly darts out her tongue and licks* SAM*'s hand,
>slowly.*

>SAM *is alarmed. Frozen.*

>*Then—so is* ADA.

>*Beat.*

>*Beat.*

>*They stay frozen, looking at each other.*

>*A beat.*

>*Then—*

ADA

Um.

SAM

Okay.

ADA

Um.

SAM

Well . . .

ADA

Yeah . . .

SAM

Okay, so this is a moment in which . . .

ADA

In which . . . ?

SAM

In which we can decide . . .

ADA

Right, decide . . .

SAM

Decide whether it is weird . . .

ADA

(Catching her drift.)
Right, or . . . not . . . weird . . .

SAM

Right, and so let's decide . . .

ADA

Let's both decide . . .

> *Beat.*
>
> *Beat.*
>
> *Beat.*

ADA & SAM

Not.

SAM

(Smiling.)
Not.

ADA

(Smiling.)
Not!

SAM

Good.

ADA

Okay. Good.

> *Beat. They smile at each other.*

SAM

(Blurting it out.)
Do you love me more than Dorrie?

ADA

What?

SAM

(Instantly mortified.)
Nothing.

> SAM*'s eyes start to well up.*

She looks away from ADA.

ADA *holds her gaze on* SAM.

Beat. Then–

SAM *coughs.*

ADA

Bless you. . . .

SAM

Thanks.

ADA

Are you okay?

SAM *rubs her eyes.*

SAM

My contact lenses.

ADA

Maybe you should get new contact lens solution.

ADA *gets up and starts to walk away.*

Before she can leave—

SAM *sobs, once—loudly.*

She immediately tries to pretend it didn't happen.

ADA

. . . Sam . . .?

SAM

(Highly defensive.)
It was a cough!!!

ADA

Sam what's wrong???

A beat. SAM *weeps.*

SAM

Oh Ada. . . .
(Weeps.)
I want to *die* . . .!
(She weeps.)
I want to die . . . so bad . . .!

ADA *looks at her. A beat. Then—*

ADA

(Softly.)

You can't say stuff like that, Sam. . . .

SAM

But it's *true . . .!*

ADA

But you still can't . . . *say* it . . .! People will think . . .

(Beat.)

. . . you're a . . . freak. . . .

SAM *weeps.*

ADA

Don't say stuff like that.

(Beat.)

Don't think it.

(Beat.)

Just . . .

(Beat; considers . . .)

. . . be happy . . .! All the time. Like me!

(She laughs, to demonstrate how happy she is.)

Hahahahaha!!!

ADA *begins practicing ballet moves; she sings, softly, to herself.*

ADA

(Singing to herself.)

. . . *I just can't help . . . but think I am . . .*

SAM *weeps.* ADA *looks at her.*

A beat. Then–

ADA

Do you want a tissue . . .?

Beat.

SAM

No.

(Beat; darkly.)

I'm *happy.*

Beat.

ADA

(Brightly.)

Good!

> SAM *continues to cry.*

> *A beat. Then—*

> *The phone rings. They look at it.*

ADA

I'll get it. It's probably for me.

> *(Beat.)*

I'm gonna pick it up in the other room.

> *(Beat; pointedly.)*

I would like the privacy.

> ADA *prances into the other room.*

> SAM *stares at the phone as it continues to ring.*

> *A beat. Then—*

> ADA *picks up the phone in the other room.*

ADA

(From the other room.)

Hello? . . .

> *(Beat.)*

Hey D. "*Whaddup?*"

> SAM *picks up the phone in the kitchen and listens to* ADA
> *and* DORRIE *'s conversation.*

ADA

Hahaha wouldn't it be funny if I actually talked like that? Hahahaha.
"WHADDUP???" Hahahahaha.

> *(Beat.)*

Okay it wasn't that funny stop laughing so much.

> SAM *rubs her eyes; stops crying. Listens with laser-sharp*
> *focus.*

ADA

Uh-huh . . .?

> *(Beat.)*

Uh-huh . . .????

> *(Beat.)*

Okay I love you so much!

>   *(Beat.)*

Forever and ever.

>   *(Beat.)*

And ever and EVER!! HAHAHAHAHAHAHA!!!

>   SAM *slowly hangs up the phone as* ADA *continues to laugh on the phone with* DORRIE.
>
>   SAM*'s eyes fix with a steely resolve.*

SCENE 4

SAM *and* DORRIE *at softball practice. They wait to go up at bat.*

SAM *spits on the ground.*

SAM

You're my sister's friend.

DORRIE

Sorry?

SAM

YOU'RE MY SISTER'S FRIEND???

DORRIE

Oh. Yeah. I guess. Am I?

SAM

I don't know. She talks about you.

DORRIE

She does?

SAM

Yeah.

DORRIE

What does she say?

SAM

You're up.

DORRIE

What?

SAM

You're up at bat?

DORRIE

(Panicking.)

Oh!

DORRIE *jumps up, runs offstage. After some moments . . . she comes back.*

DORRIE

(Confused.)

I wasn't up at bat.

SAM *spits.*

                    SAM

I know.

                    DORRIE

Why did you say I was?

                    SAM

It was a joke. I guess you don't have a very good sense of humor.

                    DORRIE

Oh.

      Beat.

                    SAM

You're up at bat.

                    DORRIE

No I'm not.

                    SAM

No, you really are this time.

                    DORRIE

Okay.

      DORRIE *exits.*

      Then, she comes back. She just sits down.

      SAM *spits.*

      DORRIE *closes her eyes and opens her palms, rests them
      on her knees.*

                    SAM

You weren't up at bat that time either, were you?

      DORRIE *doesn't respond.*

                    SAM

What are you doing?

                    DORRIE

Meditating.

                    SAM

That's so gay.

      DORRIE *ignores her, keeps meditating.*

                    SAM

How do you know how to do that?

                    DORRIE
        (Her eyes still closed.)
I learned it in therapy.

                    SAM
You go to *therapy???*

                    DORRIE
My doctor thinks my acne might be stress-related, so I go to therapy.

        (Beat; opens her eyes.)
I have stress-related childhood acne.

                    SAM
I don't even know what to say to that.

        DORRIE *resumes meditating.*

        A beat. Then—

                    SAM
You should stay away from my sister, you know.

        DORRIE *keeps meditating.*

                    SAM
HEY. <u>Pay attention</u>.

        Beat. DORRIE *opens one eye.*

                    SAM
Why does she like you???

                    DORRIE
I don't know.

                    SAM
That's what I thought.

        Beat.

        DORRIE *resumes meditating.*

        SAM *watches. Spits.*

        A beat.

        Then–

                    SAM
I think we got off on the wrong foot. I'm Sam.

        SAM *extends her hand to* DORRIE.

                    DORRIE
        (Opens one eye, extends her hand.)
I'm Dorrie.

They shake hands.

A beat. Then—

DORRIE *looks off.*

> DORRIE

I think you're up at bat.

> SAM

Very funny. I like that—a girl with wit.

> DORRIE

No, seriously, you're really up at bat, I think.

> SAM

Oh really???

> *(Looks up.)*

Oh fuck, I am! Shit!

> SAM *runs off.*

> DORRIE *smiles to herself. A beat. Then—*

> SAM *comes jogging back.*

> SAM

> *(Out of breath.)*

I just want you to know—before I go up at bat: I'm not your friend. I'm just keeping an eye on you.

> *(Beat.)*

For my sister.

> DORRIE

Okay.

> SAM

Okay.

> *(Beat.)*

Good.

> SAM *jogs away.*

> *A beat.* DORRIE *smiles to herself.*

> DORRIE

> *(Softly, to herself:)*

Now I have two.

SCENE 5

The voices of three girls scream: **_"TEENAGERS!!!"_**

> ADA _and_ DORRIE _sit in front of their laptops, at_ DORRIE_'s house._

> _The girls are now seventeen. They wear different uniforms._ ADA_'s skirt is rolled up even higher. She wears several long strings of beads._

ADA

Lemme see yours.

DORRIE

It's not finished.

ADA

Lemme _see_ it.

DORRIE

No!

ADA

Come _on!_

DORRIE

Ada . . .!

> ADA _shoves her face right in front of_ DORRIE_'s face._

ADA

DORRIE!

> DORRIE _is looking at_ ADA_'s face; she seems entranced. . . ._

DORRIE

> _(Almost involuntarily.)_

Wow. . . .

ADA

> _(Pulling away, slightly.)_

What.

DORRIE

I was just—your eyes . . . they're so—_big_. . . . You're so . . . _pretty_ . . .

ADA

Really?

DORRIE

(Somewhat embarrassed.)

Yeah.

ADA

Awww! Thanks.

ADA *wraps her arms around* DORRIE *and squeezes her, tight.*

DORRIE *beams, and giggles like a little schoolgirl.*

DORRIE

Mmmm . . . it feels so good when you hold me, Ada, just like this. . . .

DORRIE *nuzzles her head into* ADA*'s bosom.*

ADA

(Absently; creeping her hand toward DORRIE*'s laptop.)*

Mmmm, I know . . . it feels so gooooood, right . . .?

Suddenly, ADA *snatches* DORRIE*'s laptop.*

ADA

(Snatching laptop.)

Yoinkers!

DORRIE

(Alarmed.)

Ada!

ADA

I'm gonna read it one way or another, Dorrie, so you might as well just let me, now.

DORRIE

(Miserable.)

Fine.

ADA

(Cheerfully.)

Ha ha, I always win.

ADA *begins to read from* DORRIE*'s laptop.*

ADA

"My College Essay: By Dorrie Wasserman"—great title, Dorrie, haha— "If I had to describe one pivotal experience in my short life, it would be the moment I met . . ." oh my god. . . .

DORRIE

(Mortified.)
Oh no.

ADA

It's. . . about. . .

(Beat.)
me . . .!

DORRIE
(Hiding her face in her hands.)
I want to die I want to die I want to die I want to *die . . .!*

ADA *throws her arms around* DORRIE.

ADA

Oh Dorrie, you *angel*—you absolute *angel . . .!*

DORRIE *begins to cry.*

DORRIE

Oh Ada—I'm so *embarrassed . . .!*

ADA *ignores her, continues reading aloud.* DORRIE*'s face grows redder and redder.*

ADA

"I never thought I could be friends with Ada. She was the pinnacle of perfection"—oh, Dorrie!—"and I had long suffered social ostracism as a result of having debilitating childhood acne and many other humiliating ailments."

(Beat; considers. . .)
Well . . . I don't think you need to tell the colleges *that.* . . .

DORRIE
(Softly.)
My college advisor said it would breed sympathy. . . .

(Beat. ADA *considers. . . .)*

ADA

I didn't think of that. . . .

A beat. ADA *skims through the rest of the essay.*

ADA

Wow, this is—aside from the stupid font you used—this is really amazing. . . .

DORRIE

(With some pride.)

Thank you.

Beat.

ADA

Give it to me.

DORRIE

What?

ADA

Give me your essay.

DORRIE

(Doom setting in.)

Ada . . . .

ADA

(A threat.)

Dorrie.

DORRIE

(Nearly choking on her own voice.)

Ada. Please . . .!

ADA

Dorrie? I've given you so much. What have you ever *given me???*

DORRIE

(Beat; she tries not to cry.)

I love that essay. I worked hard on it. My mom already *proofread* it . . .!

ADA *begins to twirl a strand of* DORRIE *'s hair around her finger, affectionately.*

ADA

(Twirling DORRIE *'s hair; sweetly.)*

Write another essay about, oh I don't know, any of your other problems. You have *soooooo* many problems, Dorrie. I don't have *anything* to write about that will help me garner sympathy.

DORRIE

(Almost a croak.)

Ada. . . .

Beat. ADA *stops twirling* DORRIE *'s hair.*

ADA

I will never be your friend if you don't do this for me.

DORRIE

(Goes white.)

Ada . . .!

ADA

I will never *speak* to you again.

DORRIE

(Cries.)

Ada—*please* . . .!

Now, ADA *begins to cry.*

ADA

I'm so scared, Dorrie! I'm so scared I won't get in! That place is my *dream* school . . .! And *you'll* get in, and *Sam* will get in, and what will happen to *me* . . .?! Everyone will leave me and I'll be stuck in my house all alone with no one to love me, and—

She chokes on her own sobs. She sobs.

DORRIE *reaches out a hand and rubs her back.*

DORRIE

Oh, Ada. . . .

A beat. Then—

DORRIE

(Gulps; wiping away her tears.)

You can have it, Ada. I'll write another essay. It won't take long.

(Gulps; wipes away tears; smiles.)

<u>You can have it.</u>

ADA

(Gleeful.)

Oh, *thank* you, Dorrie!

ADA *lunges for* DORRIE *and wraps her in her arms. She covers* DORRIE*'s face with kisses—then pulls away.*

ADA

Euuugh. Your face tastes terrible.

DORRIE

(Glumly.)

It's my acne medication.

ADA

Well. . . look, Dorrie. This is how much I love you.

ADA protrudes her tongue and licks DORRIE*'s face, from her chin up to her hairline, slowly.* DORRIE *can't help but beam.*

ADA

Sam would never do something this selfless for me. You've taken this friendship . . . to the next level.

DORRIE

Oh, Ada! You don't know how happy you make me!

Beat. They smile at each other.

ADA

Now!

(Hands DORRIE*'s laptop back to her.)*

Start changing the name "Ada" to "Dorrie," so it's from my perspective, 'K?

DORRIE

(Almost excited, now.)

Okay . . .!

ADA

(Gathering her belongings,)

And send it to me when you're done. I'm gonna go hang out with Sam.

DORRIE

But, Ada—

ADA

Love you forever and ever!!

She kisses DORRIE *on top of her head, and skips out of there.*

ADA

(Singing to herself cheerfully.)

Ha-ha-ha-ha-HA-ha. . .!

DORRIE *looks after her. Then, she turns back to her computer.*

Her eyes fix with a steely resolve.

She types.

SCENE 6

ADA *and* SAM *at their kitchen table. They wear pretty spring dresses.* SAM *wears a graduation cap.* ADA *looks like she has been crying. She has a graduation cap in front of her.*

There is a bottle of whiskey on the table.

ADA
(Hoarsely.)
You could at least take your stupid cap off.

SAM
(Taking it off.)
Sorry.
(Beat.)

SAM
I thought it would be funny to leave—

ADA
(Cutting her off.)
It's not.

SAM
Sorry.

A beat. SAM *takes her cap off. They stare at the whiskey bottle.*

SAM
I understand you're in pain.
(Beat; she reaches her hand across the table and puts it over ADA*'s hand)*
You're not alone. . . .

ADA
(Jerking her hand away.)
Lesbo.

SAM
(Stung.)
Hey.

A beat. They stare at the whiskey bottle.

ADA

(Snorts.)

I should have known. I *should have known . . .!* You got in and Dorrie got waitlisted and I got fucking *rejected.* Isn't that alllllways the way it is. Everyone thinks the pretty girls get it all. Really all we get is shit. *Shit.* We eat shit our whole lives and we wipe it off our mouths like the ladies we are, but really, all we're doing is eating *shit,* day in and day out, our whole goddamn lives. . . .

(Beat.)

SAM

(Softly.)

Come on, Ada. It's okay. Let's just go to Dorrie's stupid graduation party and get it over with.

ADA *starts to cry.*

ADA

(Hanging her head in her hands; weeping.)

That school was all I wanted! I can't believe you're going there. . .!

A beat. Then—

ADA

Don't go there.

SAM

Ada. . . .

ADA

(Crying pathetically.)

Go anywhere else! Just not *there!* I can't *live* with it if you go there . . .!

SAM

(Softly.)

P.F. Touchane teaches there. He's my hero, Ada.

ADA

You're not even a very good artist.

(Beat.)

SAM

(With conviction.)

Yes, I am.

ADA

I've seen your stuff. It's cheap. It's all about Mom and what a drunk she is. Wah wah, build a bridge and get *over* it.

SAM *gets up and crosses to the kitchen cupboard.*

> SAM
> *(Soft, but firm.)*

I write about what I know.

> SAM *takes a glass out of the cupboard, crosses to the*
> *refrigerator and takes out a glass bottle of milk. She pops*
> *the top off, and pours some milk into the glass.*

> ADA
> *(Emotional.)*

How do you think *Mom* would feel about you exploiting her like that?

> SAM

I don't care how she feels—she's not a good mom and she knows it.

> ADA
> *(Suddenly very emotional.)*

You have to *care* for sick people, Sam! You can't just let them *die . . .!*

> ADA *weeps, at a loss. She hangs her head in her hands.* SAM
> *sips her milk, watches her sister.*

> ADA

Oh god. Oh, *god . . .!*

> SAM *looks at her sister, then looks at the bottle of whiskey*
> *on the table.*

> SAM
> *(Softly.)*

Why don't you just drink it . . .?

> ADA
> *(Weeps.)*

I'm *scared . . .!*

> SAM

I don't think it's that big of a deal.

> ADA

How would you know? You've never drank either.

> SAM

I know it makes Mom feel better when *she* wants to die. . . .

> ADA

I don't "want to *die,*" Sam—I'm not a fucking *freak.* . . .

> ADA *hangs her head in her hands.*

> SAM *watches, in pain.*

SAM

I *hate* seeing you so sad.

(Beat.)

It'll help. I promise.

ADA *looks up, stares at the whiskey bottle.*

A beat. Then—

ADA

I'm gonna drink it.

SAM

Good.

ADA

Have some with me.

A beat; SAM *considers. . . .*

SAM

Okay. But you can have most of it. You're sadder.

ADA

Thanks.

SAM *gets a new glass out of the cupboard, pours some milk into the new glass.*

ADA *takes the whiskey, unscrews the cap, smells it.*

SAM

We can even bring some with us to the party, in a water bottle—I've seen Mom do that.

SAM *pours some whiskey into* ADA*'s glass of milk, then pours a tiny bit into her own glass.*

ADA

I need more.

SAM

Really?

ADA

If I'm gonna get drunk, I might as well get really drunk.

SAM *pours more whiskey into* ADA*'s glass of milk.*

ADA

Thanks.

SAM

Cheers.

ADA

Cheers.

They cheers. Then—

They both drink.

SAM *shudders and puts her glass down after a sip.*

ADA *drains her glass.*

A beat. Then—

SAM

How do you feel . . .?

Beat. ADA *considers. . . .*

ADA

(A new light in her eyes.)

Like an adult.

SCENE 7

DORRIE's *kitchen. The space is decorated with pink and blue balloons that say "CONGRATULATIONS DORRIE!" on them; music and laughter are heard from outside. It is late afternoon—dusk is falling.*

ADA, *alone, leans against the kitchen counter, with a water bottle, which is filled with a milky brown liquid. She takes a swig. She puts it down. She begins to do a dance. It is a strange, twisty, balletic dance. She incorporates some of the moves we saw her do as a ten-year-old. She dances slowly at first, then begins to pick up steam. She becomes increasingly graceful, even daring high jumps and challenging spins. She sings to herself softly as she dances.*

ADA
. . . you've got a friend in me . . . you've got a friend in me . . .!

Eventually, worn out, she stops dancing; She pants. She leans her hands on her knees, tries to catch her breath. She straightens up, and wobbles a bit as she lunges for her water bottle. She takes a deep swig from the water bottle. She looks at the air in front of her, her gaze cloudy.

A beat. Then—

DORRIE *flies in.*

DORRIE
(Surprised.)
Oh, Ada!

ADA
Dorrie.

DORRIE
(Faltering.)
I—I didn't know you were . . . in here. . . .

ADA
(Cutting her off; slurring her words a bit.)
I'm just resting. . . .

(Beat.)

DORRIE

Are you all right . . .? Ada . . .?

ADA *lifts her head, heavily. She fixes her gaze on* DORRIE, *blearily.*

ADA

(Still slurring, slightly.)
I'm *fantastic.*

A beat. DORRIE *looks at* ADA. *She hesitates, then moves closer to her.*

DORRIE

(Gulps.)
Ada.

ADA

(Thickly.)
What.

DORRIE

I need to—tell you . . . something. . . .

A beat. ADA *looks at* DORRIE—*her gaze cloudy, but somehow focused.*

ADA

What.

DORRIE *whimpers, softly.*

DORRIE

(Tiny voice.)
Oh, Ada. . . . I'm so scared!

ADA

(Heavily.)
You got in.

DORRIE *begins to cry.*

DORRIE

Oh, Ada. . . .

ADA

You got in off the waitlist. Didn't you. You got in.

A terrible, heavy beat.

DORRIE *just looks at* ADA, *and cries. Then—*

She nods.

A beat. Then—

ADA *slams her hands down on* DORRIE*'s shoulders and stares at her.*

DORRIE *shakes, petrified.*

A beat. Then—

ADA *pulls* DORRIE *into a fierce, tight hug.* DORRIE *trembles with relief.*

> DORRIE

Oh! Ada . . .!

> DORRIE *relaxes, hugs* ADA *back.*

> DORRIE
> *(Voice trembling.)*

You're—you're not m-mad?

> ADA

No. I'm not.

> DORRIE
> *(Joyously relieved.)*

I thought you'd be so m-mad . . . at me . . .!

> ADA
> *(Realizing it for the first time.)*

I don't care anymore. I. Don't. Care.

> ADA *releases her hold on* DORRIE *but keeps her hands on* DORRIE*'s shoulders.*

> ADA

Oh, Dorrie—It's the strangest *thing* . . .!

> *(Beat; considers . . .)*

. . . It's so *wonderful* . . .!

> *(She giggles like a little girl.)*

I just don't care about a darn thing!

> *(Begins to dance again.)*

I *just* . . . *don't* . . . *care* . . .!

> DORRIE
> *(A little scared.)*

Are you a-all right, Ada?

ADA

Congratulations, Dorrie. I wish you all the luck in the world!

ADA *plants two hard, wet kisses on* DOORIE *'s cheeks.* DOORIE *beams.*

DORRIE

Oh! I'm so happy you're not mad at me, Ada . . .!

ADA

(A sudden pang of guilt—a sudden moment of clarity.)

Ohhh. . . . I'm so mean, aren't I?

DORRIE

(Panicking.)

Mean? No, you're not mean. You're—you. There's no one else *like* you. That's why everyone wants to be around you, all the time!

ADA

(Suddenly beginning to cry.)

No one wants to be around me all the time! I don't even have any *friends*, besides you and *Sam* . . .!

DORRIE

(Trying desperately to soothe her.)

Well that's because you—*intimidate* people, Ada . . .!

(Beat; she strokes ADA*'s hair.)*

You *shine*. . . . Like a *star . . .!*

A beat.

ADA

(Wiping tears away.)

Really?

DORRIE *nods, sweetly.*

DORRIE

(Wiping away ADA*'s tears, gently.)*

You'll be a *huge* success in college! And I do believe there's a reason for everything—my meditation practice tells me so. There's a reason you're meant to go . . . wherever you go.

A beat. ADA *takes a swig from her water bottle.*

DORRIE

What are you drinking?

ADA

Milk.

DORRIE

In a . . . water bottle . . .??

> *Beat.*

ADA

Uh-huh.

DORRIE

Why's it brown???

ADA

I dunno.

> *Beat.*

DORRIE

Okay.

> *(Beat.)*

Oh Ada, we're both going to be so happy—I *know* it! And now Sam and I can really get to know each other. Now we can all *three* be friends. Sam and Ada and Dorrie . . .!

> ADA *teeters.*

ADA

> *(Stumbling.)*

. . . Dorrie. . . .

DORRIE

Oh! Do you not feel well, Ada . . .?

ADA

> *(Slurring her words.)*

I don'tfeelthat well. . . .

DORRIE

Drink something.

ADA

I will.

> ADA *swigs from her water bottle.*

DORRIE

> *(Burrowing herself in* ADA*'s bosom.)*

Oh, Ada. I love you more and more each day.

ADA

> *(Absently patting* DORRIE*'s head.)*

Thank you, D—

Before she can get the word out, ADA *throws up . . . on*
DORRIE.

ADA *laughs.*

DORRIE

Oh no, Ada—you're sick! Lemme—lemme get you a. . . .

*DORRIE grabs a handkerchief out of her pocket and begins
to try to wipe the vomit off* ADA*'s face.*

ADA *keeps laughing—she throws her arms up in the air
and begins spinning, and singing to herself.*

ADA

(Sings.)

*I jusssst . . . can't help . . . but think I am . . . extreeeemely . . . beeeaauuut-
ifullll . . . !*

DORRIE continues to try to wipe ADA*'s vomit off* ADA*'s face
while* ADA *spins.*

DORRIE

I'll go get Sam—and tell her to take you home, Ada. She'll put you to
bed. . . .

ADA *stops spinning.*

She leans both hands on DORRIE*'s shoulders to steady
herself.*

She looks into DORRIE*'s eyes with absolute conviction.*

ADA

(A spirited whisper.)

You don't understand, do you? Dorrie, Dorrie—you big old fool . . .!
Oh Dorrie . . .

(Beat; she stares right into DORRIE*'s terrified eyes:)*

I'm *just getting started!*

SCENE 8

DORRIE*'s kitchen, several hours later. It is now dark out-side.*

DORRIE *is cleaning up the remnants of her party. She hums contentedly to herself as she cleans.*

A beat. Then—

SAM *enters* DORRIE*'s kitchen, quietly. She has a pencil tucked behind her ear.* DORRIE *doesn't see her.* SAM *observes* DORRIE *for a moment. Then—*

SAM

Hello, Dorrie.

DORRIE *wheels around, surprised.*

DORRIE

(Sort of scared.)

Oh! Sam . . .! I didn't know—you were—didn't you . . . go home . . .? With Ada . . .?

SAM

I thought you might need some help cleaning up.

DORRIE

Oh.

(Sort of queasily.)

Thank you. . . .

SAM *begins to help* DORRIE *clean.*

They work in silence.

A beat. Then—

SAM

Have a fun party?

DORRIE

Oh, sure. It was super . . . fun. . . .

(Beat.)

Did you have fun . . .?

                              SAM

Sure.

        (Hops off her chair.)

Loads of it.

        SAM *picks up a balloon that has fallen to the ground,
        studies it. . . .*

                              DORRIE

        (Weakly.)

Yaaaay. . . .

        SAM *surreptiously removes the pencil from behind her ear.*

                              SAM

Too bad about my sister, though, huh?

        SAM *suddenly stabs the balloon with the pencil—pops it.*

                              DORRIE

        (Startled.)

Ow!

        (Beat; recovering.)

Yeah. How's she doing?

        SAM *picks up another balloon, and studies it.*

                              SAM

Well, I took her home, and . . . she's sleeping. Like an angel. Poor
thing.

                              DORRIE

        (Uneasy.)

I—I don't know why she . . . got sick . . . so suddenly. . . . I feel . . . so
bad. . . . I hope she had an okay time . . . anyway. . . .

                              SAM

Oh I'm sure she had a blast.

        SAM *pops the balloon;* DORRIE *flinches.*

                              SAM

Hey listen, Dorrie. Here's the thing: Ada told me your great news. I'm
so happy for you. But here's the thing: Ada's not so happy. And here's
the other thing: Neither am I. And here's the *last thing :* Even though
we'll be going to the same college in the fall? I need you to know this:
I will not speak to you. I will not *look* at you. You will be *dead* to me. Do
you understand?

A beat. DORRIE *tries not to cry.*

SAM

Do. You. Under. Stand???

DORRIE

What's—what's *wrong*, Sam . . .?

SAM

(Very calm.)

What's wrong . . .?

(Then—erupts:)

What's WRONG?!? *Look what you did to her, Dorrie!* *LOOK WHAT YOU DID!!!*

DORRIE

(Whimpering.)

I didn't . . . do *anything* . . .! Sam. . . .

SAM

(An ice cold threat.)

Don't speak to my sister. Don't *speak* to her. *Ever. Again.*

DORRIE

(Weeping.)

She's—

SAM

(Deadly.)

What.

DORRIE

(Blubbering.)

She's—*my friend* . . .!

SAM

Oh, she is? Well that's so *weird*, Dorrie, 'cause you FUCKED her. You *fucked* her over, today. And you're too __STUPID__ to even know you were doing it.

DORRIE

(Hysterical.)

She knew I applied to that school, too . . .! We never thought it'd be— you and me going there, without her . . .! I didn't—

(Barely able to get the words out.)

I didn't *know* . . .!

SAM *picks up a new balloon and studies it, as she crosses to* DORRIE.

SAM
(Calm, now; almost sweet.)
Oh, of course you didn't. . . .

(Approaches DORRIE, *with balloon in her hand; in a honeyed tone:)*
Dear, dear, *sweet* . . . Dorrie. You never know what you're doing, do you . . .?

SAM *strokes* DORRIE*'s hair, by* DORRIE*'s ear, with her hand that holds the pencil.*

DORRIE *stands there and lets her—whimpering, trembling, terrified.*

Slowly, SAM *lifts her other hand, with the balloon in it, to the other side of* DORRIE*'s head.*

SAM
(Lifting balloon.)
Shhh . . . shhh. . . . It's okay, Dorrie. It's okay. As long as you stay away, it's alllll gonna be okay. . . .

SAM *twirls a strand of* DORRIE*'s hair around her finger, almost affectionately.* DORRIE *stares in front of her, crying, shaking, silent.*

A beat. Then—

SAM *slams the pencil into the balloon, right next to* DORRIE*'s ear.*

DORRIE *screams.*

Blackout.

SCENE 9

*The voices of three girls scream: **"YOUNG ADULTHOOD!!!"***

> *We hear the sounds of hands slapping against each other.*
>
> *Lights creep up on* DORRIE *and* SAM, *in a dungeon-like dorm room.*
>
> *They play a hand game—very intensely, and very rapidly.*
>
> *They play it as if their lives depended on it.*
>
> *They play it for a long, long time.*
>
> *After several rounds,* DORRIE *messes up, and the game falls apart.*

SAM

You messed up, that was six.

DORRIE

I'm sorry, I thought it was five.

SAM

Yeah, I could see you did.

> *Beat.*

DORRIE

Do you want to play again . . .?

SAM

No. I don't.

> *Beat.*

SAM

There's nothing to do in this stupid, stinking *dorm*.

DORRIE

I know.

SAM

You're just saying that 'cause I said it.

DORRIE

Yeah.

*Beat. Then—*DORRIE *gets an idea.*

DORRIE

Let's talk about boys???

SAM

(Reluctantly.)

Okay.

DORRIE

Who do you like?!?

SAM

No one.

DORRIE

Me neither.

SAM

There aren't any cute ones.

DORRIE

No.

SAM

And even if they are. . . .

DORRIE

Right.

SAM

None of them like me.

DORRIE

Right.

SAM

(Suddenly defensive.)

What do you mean?!

DORRIE

Um.

SAM

You think they don't like me???

DORRIE

No, I bet they do.

SAM

I don't care.

Beat.

> DORRIE

I like you.

> SAM

I don't care.

> *Beat.*

> *Then—*DORRIE *gets an idea.*

> DORRIE

Should we paint our nails, or do something girly like that???

> SAM

Yeah.

> *(Gets a really good idea.)*

Except let's paint our bodies!

> DORRIE

> *(Confused.)*

Okay. . . .

> SAM

> *(Really excited.)*

Let's paint them so it looks like we're *bleeding*, and then go out into the hall and *scare* everyone!!!

> DORRIE

> *(Really apprehensive.)*

That's scary. . . .

> SAM

Yeah, that's the point.

> DORRIE

Sorry.

> SAM

I have red nail polish—that's the only thing I have that could look like blood.

> DORRIE

> *(Incredibly nervous.)*

Okay. . . .

> SAM

Okay! Let me find it.

> *She finds it.*

Okay I found it.

(Almost giddy with excitement.)
I'm gonna do you first.

DORRIE

Okay.

SAM

I'm gonna do, just like, a nosebleed, to start. . . .

DORRIE

Right.

SAM

Actually I'm gonna do a nose-*gush*.

DORRIE

Huh.

SAM

I'm gonna make it look like your whole *brain's* coming out of your nose!!!

DORRIE
(Tiny, terrified voice.)
. . . aaaaahhhh . . .!

SAM

Hold still.

> SAM *paints on* DORRIE*'s nose with the nail polish. She paints a lot of red nail polish under* DORRIE*'s nose and some kind of on her cheeks and on her chin.*

DORRIE

Oh, wow. . . .

SAM

What?

DORRIE

It smells.

SAM

Well, you know nail polish smells.

DORRIE

I know. I've just never had it . . .
(Beat; considers . . .)
So close to my nose . . . before. . . .

SAM
(Nodding compassionately.)
I know what you mean.

(She finishes.)

There, all done.

> SAM *puts the nail polish away.*

DORRIE

How does it look.

SAM

It looks so fucked up. It looks great.

DORRIE

(Hugely anxious.)

Yaaaay. . . .

SAM

Now go out into the hall and ask for help.

DORRIE

Okay. . . .

SAM

Go!!!

DORRIE

What do I say???

SAM

"Help! *Help*!!!"

DORRIE

(Beyond petrified.)

Okay. . . .

> DORRIE *goes out into the hall, offstage.*

DORRIE

(Offstage; kind of lamely.)

Help. . . . Help!

> *A beat.*

> DORRIE *waits. Then—*

> *She peeks her head back in—looks at* SAM *like, "Well, I tried."*

> SAM *silently gestures to her that she needs to amp up the intensity with the "Help"s.*

> DORRIE *goes back out in the hall.*

DORRIE

(More desperate.)

Help!

(Beat.)

Help!!!

(Beat; really desperately.)

Help!!! HELP!!! HEEELLLLLLLLPPPPPPP!!!

(Insanely distressed.)

HEEEELLLLLLLPPPPPPPPPPPPPP!!! HELP HELP HELP HELP HELP HELP HELP HELP HELP HELP HELP HELP HELP HELP HELP HELP HEEEELLLLIIIIIIIIIIIIIIIIIIIIIIIIIIIIILLLPPPPPPPPPPPPPP!!!!!!!! OHMYGOD I'M DYING PLEASE HELP MEEEEEEE HELLP!!!!!!!!!!!!!!!!!!!!

Beat. Then—

DORRIE *comes back in the room.*

DORRIE

(In despair.)

No one helped me.

SAM

(Also in despair.)

I know.

SAM *curls up on the floor.* DORRIE *looks at* SAM.

A beat. Then—

DORRIE

Sam?

SAM

What.

DORRIE

Do you have any nail polish remover . . .?

SAM

(Eyes closed.)

No.

DORRIE *tries to peel the nail polish off her face.*

DORRIE

Maybe I can peel it off.

Beat.

DORRIE

Sam?

SAM

What.

> DORRIE

I'm so bored.

> *Beat.*

> DORRIE *continues to try to peel the nail polish off her face.*

> DORRIE

Sam?

> SAM

What.

> DORRIE

What do you think . . . Ada's doing? Right now??

> *Beat.* SAM *doesn't say anything.*

> DORRIE

Sam???

> *Suddenly,* DORRIE *realizes that* SAM *is crying, softly.*

> DORRIE

Oh . . .!

> SAM

Go *away.*

> DORRIE

What?

> SAM

Get away from me!

> DORRIE

Sam . . .!

> SAM

Get out of my room, Dorrie!!!

> DORRIE

No, Sam—you're *sad* . . .!

> SAM *weeps.*

> DORRIE *approaches her, gently, and puts her arms around her.*

> SAM

<u>*Get AWAY from me, I said! You FOOL!!!*</u>

> SAM *shoves* DORRIE *away from her—hard.*

DORRIE

Ow!

SAM

I *told* you!

DORRIE

(Really sad.)

Oh, Sam. . . .

SAM *cries, and cries.*

DORRIE *starts crying too.*

DORRIE

I hate seeing you so sad! It makes me so sad, too . . .!

(Beat; cries.)

Why are we so sad???

(Beat; cries.)

I want to be happy again . . .!

DORRIE *cries.* SAM *weeps.*

A beat. SAM *considers.* . . . *Then—*

SAM

Dorrie—something happened. With Ada. After your graduation party. . . .
Something terrible. Something that. . . .

She cries and cries; can't finish.

DORRIE

(Her heart breaking.)

Oh, Sam. You can tell me . . .! Dorrie won't judge you. Dorrie will only
love you. Dorrie will only *listen* . . .!

SAM

(Hysterical.)

I want to die. I want to die . . . *so bad . . .!*

DORRIE

(With deep compassion.)

I know.

(Trying to be helpful.)

I want to die too . . .!

Beat.

SAM

(Wiping tears away.)

You—you do . . .?

DORRIE

(Nodding enthusiastically.)

Oh often—yes!

SAM

(Suddenly a bit more hopeful.)

Really . . .?!

DORRIE

Oh, *yes!*

(Giggling impishly.)

I used to fantasize I would get shot in the head by a sniper on the escalator at the mall . . .!

SAM

(Amazed.)

I used to fantasize I would get raped and tortured by all my favorite *cartoon characters* at a banquet *feast . . .!*

DORRIE

(Excited.)

I used to lick my lips and then put *ice* cubes on them and then *rip* them off so my lips would bleed and *bleed !!!*

SAM

(Incredibly excited, also.)

I used to peel all the skin off my lips until they bled and bled and then I would stick pieces of *paper* to my lips and then *rip* them off so they would bleed even *more* and then I would *SAVE THEM !!!*

The girls laugh and laugh.

SAM & DORRIE

HAHAHAHAHAHAHA!!!

(Beat.)

SAM

(Smiling at DORRIE*)*

Ada thinks I'm a freak.

DORRIE

No, she doesn't. . . .

SAM

Yes she does. She tells me it's not normal to—to think stuff . . . like that. . . .

                              DORRIE
Well. . . .

          (Beat; considers . . .)
Maybe it's not *normal*, but. . . .

          (With a generous smile; taking SAM*'s hand:)*
You're not *alone* . . .!

          A beat. SAM *looks at* DORRIE. *Smiles, tears in her eyes.*

                              SAM
          (Deeply moved.)
Thank you, Dorrie.

                              DORRIE
Thank you, Sam.
          Beat.

                              SAM
You're a good friend, Dorrie.
          (Beat.)
You've taken this friendship . . . to the next level. . . .

                              DORRIE
Oh Sam! You don't know how happy you make me . . .!

          DORRIE *beams at* SAM, *tears in her eyes.* SAM *beams back
          at* DORRIE.

          A joyful moment.

          Then—

                              SAM
          (With some hesitation.)
Can I—can I . . . draw you . . .? Dorrie . . .?

          A beat. DORRIE*'s eyes mist over with tears of profound
          gratitude.*

                              DORRIE
          (With heartfelt sincerity.)
Nothing would give me greater pleasure.

          A beat. SAM *beams. Then—she runs and grabs her sketch-
          book and a pencil. She sits in front of* DORRIE.

                              SAM
'K—pose!

                              DORRIE
Uh. . . .

DORRIE *just stands there.*

> SAM

Like *this.*

> SAM *gets up and approaches* DORRIE. *She puts her hands on* DORRIE, *and begins to maneuver her into a pose.*

> DORRIE
>
> *(Kind of taken aback.)*

Oh . . .!

> SAM

Hold still. . . .

> DORRIE *lets* SAM *maneuver her.* SAM *maneuvers her into one of* ADA*'s strange poses.*

> SAM

Good.

> DORRIE

Is this good . . .?

> SAM

Yes. Please stop asking me to validate you.

> DORRIE

Sorry.

> SAM *stands back and inspects* DORRIE*'s pose.*

> SAM

Hmmm. . . .

> *She considers. . . . Then—she gets an idea.*

> SAM

Oh!

> SAM *runs to a drawer, and pulls out a long string of beads— the kind that* ADA *likes to wear. She runs over to* DORRIE, *and loops them around her neck.*

> *She stands back and regards* DORRIE. DORRIE *holds her pose, beams.*

> *A beat. Then—*

> SAM *begins to draw.*

> SAM
>
> *(Almost to herself.)*

You've always been sooo pretty, Dorrie. . . .

SCENE 10

DORRIE and ADA *blow up balloons at* DORRIE*'s house.*

The space is decorated with silver and gold balloons that are printed with the words "CONGRATULATIONS DORRIE!"

ADA *drinks a glass of white wine. She wears a sleek, flattering outfit, adorned with several long, elegant strings of beads.*

                              ADA
       (Blows into a balloon.)
Recently my pee has been very green.

                                   DORRIE
Oh?
       (Blows into a balloon.)
What do you think that means?

                              ADA
       (Blows into balloon.)
I think it just means I'm happy.

       They both finish blowing up their balloons; they tie them off.

       ADA *throws the balloon in the air and swats at it with her hand.*

                              ADA
God, I feel so *good*, lately!

       She makes a grand gesture with her hands; in doing so, she spills some wine on DORRIE*'s face.*

                                   DORRIE
       (Getting wine in her eye.)
Oh!

                              ADA
       (Not noticing that she spilled wine in DORRIE*'s eye.)*
'Cause I know that there's a *reason for everything*. You were *right*, Dorrie . . .!

(Takes a gulp of wine.)

I *was* a huge success in college. Maybe not in the way that . . .

(Gulps more wine; slurs her words a bit.)

. . . butlike I don'tneed to "*graduate*" in order to learn invaluable *lessons*, y'know . . .???

(More wine; swats balloon around.)

I learn more from the shit I see every *day* and the *people* I meet and all the . . . *dicks* I've fucked, and the . . .

> *She cracks herself up; drains her wine glass.* DORRIE *looks on with concern.*

DORRIE

Ada. . . .

ADA

(Swatting the balloons like crazy.)

I don't care anymore. I. Don't. *Care . . .!*

> *She tries to suck a few last drops of wine out of her glass, giggles deliriously to herself.*

DORRIE

Ada . . .?

ADA

(Swatting at a balloon; slurring her words a bit.)

Like Idunneed tohave a faggoty *graduationparty* to feel *validated* inmyself . . . y'know . . .?

DORRIE

. . . Ada. . . .

ADA

I just can't stand to be around unhappy people. If you're unhappy—do *something*, you know . . .?!

(Little gulp of wine.)

I know what *I'm* gonna *do*—'m gonna move to New York and *act* and have a glittering *life!*

DORRIE

Oh, I know you will, Ada. One day, you'll—

ADA

(Cutting her off.)

Not "*one day*," Dorrie—I'm doing it. Next month. Sooner, maybe.

DORRIE

So . . . *soon* . . . Ada . . .???

> *She looks around for the wine bottle.*

ADA

(Snorts.)

Hah! Why the fuck would I stick around *here*?!

DORRIE

Well . . . to spend the summer . . . with me . . .? And Sam . . .?

ADA

(Laughs.)

I've spent enough time with you and *Sam*, Dorrie—thanks.

> *She finds the bottle, pours the rest of it into her glass. Starts to laugh to herself.*

ADA

I mean, whaddaya *want* me to do?! Hang around this dump with *you two* and get old and *die* . . .? That's not a *life!*

(She drinks.)

I mean is that what *you* wanna do?

(Drinks.)

Is that what *Sam's* gonna do . . .?!

DORRIE

(Softly.)

Sam has her graphic novel.

ADA

(Laughs; sloppily.)

That behemoth is just sitting on a shelf collecting dust, along with her diaphragm.

DORRIE

She doesn't have a diaphragm.

ADA

I *know*, Dorrie—it's an *expression*.

DORRIE

Sorry.

> *A beat.* ADA *stares at* DORRIE.

ADA

How come you hung out with Sam, Dorrie? In college?

DORRIE

What do you . . . *mean* . . . Ada . . .?

ADA

You're *my* friend, not *Sam's.* Why would you hang out with *her??*

DORRIE

(Confused.)

Well. . . .

ADA

Was it because . . . she reminded you . . . of *me???*

DORRIE

Well . . . she's really *nice*, Ada. . . .

ADA

(Snorts.)

She's not *nice*, Dorrie! She's *Sam*, Dorrie! No one thinks she's "*nice*" . . .!

DORRIE

Well—

ADA *suddenly starts to cry.*

ADA

It's *not nice.* To hang out with each other. And not with *me . . .!* To spend four years with *each other* . . .

(Cries.)

. . . and never to think of *me . . .!*

DORRIE

But—we—oh, we thought of you all the *time, Ada . . .!* You have no *idea.* . . . Sam would even—haha!—she'd ask me to *pose* for her, the way *you* used to pose . . . and then she'd—she'd *draw* me . . .!

Beat. ADA *stiffens.*

ADA

What.

DORRIE

Oh, yes!

(Giggling.)

She would pose me, like this . . .

(She strikes a sort of heroin-chic pose.)

Or this . . .

(She strikes a sort of modern dance-y pose.)

Or this. . . .

DORRIE *strikes the sexy pose.*

> ADA
> *(Can't believe what she's seeing.)*

What??

> DORRIE
> *(Giggling mischievously.)*

Yes! And *Ada* . . . I would *wear your beads . . .!*

DORRIE *lowers herself into a chair.*

> ADA
> *(Horrified.)*

Oh my. . . *god.* . . .

DORRIE *approaches* ADA *and kneels at her feet.*

> DORRIE

Oh, Ada. . . . I can't believe you thought we weren't *thinking* of you . . .!

ADA *drinks.*

> DORRIE

You *shine.* . . . Like a *star . . .!*

ADA *drinks. She drinks. She drinks the rest of the glass of wine all at once.*

DORRIE *watches . . . with growing concern.*

A beat. Then—

> DORRIE
> *(Blurting it out, unthinking.)*

But Ada how are you going to be a successful actress when you drink so much???

A beat.

ADA *turns to look at* DORRIE *—an ice cold glare.*

DORRIE *looks back at* ADA, *goes white, with fear.* . . .

A beat. Then—

ADA *slaps* DORRIE. *Hard. Across the face.*

A beat. Then—

> DORRIE
> *(Barely audible.)*

I'm sorry. . . .

                                    ADA
Did *Sam* tell you that I drink too much?

                            DORRIE .
No-o . . .!

                                    ADA
           (Turning her back to DORRIE.*)*
She doesn't know <u>anything</u>.

                            DORRIE
           (Stammering.)
Y-you're right, Ada—I'm sure you're right . . .!

           ADA *begins to gather her stuff.*

                                    ADA
Where are you *going* . . .?!

           ADA *continues to gather her stuff.*

           In a frenzied state of hysteria, DORRIE *dives to the floor
           and grabs* ADA *by the legs.*

                            DORRIE
           (Clutching at ADA, *beginning to cry.)*
Oh, I'm just a big dummy—a big old fool . . .!

           She tightens her grip on ADA*'s legs;* ADA *struggles to break
           free.*

                            DORRIE
I'm *sorry*, Ada!

                                    ADA
           (Still struggling.)
Okay . . .!

                            DORRIE
I *love* you, Ada!

                                    ADA
           (Still struggling.)
I *know . . .!*

                            DORRIE
I <u>need you</u>, Ada . . .!

           Beat. ADA *stops struggling.*

                                    ADA
Oh, Dorrie. . . .

> ADA *relents, and lets* DORRIE *squeeze her.* ADA*'s eyes drift somewhere far away.* DORRIE *squeezes her legs, tight.*

DORRIE

Oh! Ada! Let me get you some more wine! Can I get you some more?! Let me get you some more!!

> DORRIE *unwraps herself from* ADA *and races offstage.*
>
> ADA *sits mechanically in a chair and stares at the air in front of her, her gaze cloudy and unfocused.*
>
> *A beat. Then—*
>
> DORRIE *runs back in with a new bottle of white wine.*

DORRIE

Okay, I got you some more!!!

> DORRIE *starts to pour* ADA *a new glass of wine.* ADA *stays silent—eyes far, far away.*

DORRIE

(Oblivious.)

Oh Ada, I'm so *happy . . .!*

(Finishes pouring.)

And you're going to be a huge movie star, Ada—ten feet wide, twenty feet *high . . .!*

> *(She puts an arm around* ADA *and squeezes her, tight;*
> ADA, *limply, lets her.)*

And Sam will publish her graphic *novel*, and I'll—

> *(She gets choked up thinking about how beautiful the future is going to be.)*

I'll be by your side—*always*. Both of you. Always. Forever. And ever. Sam and Ada and *Dorrie . . .!*

> ADA*'s eyes drift even further away, until they seem to just . . . deaden.*

ADA

(Slurring.)

Dorrie . . .

> DORRIE *beams at* ADA.

DORRIE

Thanks.

SCENE 11

SAM and ADA in their kitchen. They both wear black. SAM is sketching in her sketchbook. ADA is drinking a glass of white wine, and has the half-full bottle near her on the table, next to two empty wine bottles.

ADA lights a cigarette.

A beat. Then—

> SAM

Can you open the cellar door? If you're gonna smoke?

> ADA
> *(Getting up to open the cellar door.)*

I was just *about* to—don't be*little* me. . . .

> *She opens the cellar door. She looks down at the stair-case; smokes . . .*

SAM draws.

She exhales. She tries to blow a smoke ring. She fails.

A beat. Then—

> SAM
> *(Softly.)*

What did you think of the service . . .?

> ADA
> *(Ashing her cigarette.)*

I was glad Myles came. Remember him? From Ms. Sterling's class? I could tell he thought I looked hot in my mourning attire.

> *(Drag off cigarette.)*

I wanted to fuck him in the graveyard but I thought that would be too clichéd.

> *(Beat.)*

So I just gave him a blowjob instead.

> *SAM rubs her eyes.*

A beat. Then—

SAM

(Softly.)

I don't even feel sad about Mom at all.

ADA

(Chugs from wineglass; sloppily.)

Well, now you can publish your *graphic novel* about her and she'll never scream at you for it.

(Takes a sip of wine,)

Unless you believe in an afterlife.

> *She chuckles, darkly, and pours herself another glass of wine.*

SAM

You're not still planning on leaving . . . tomorrow . . .? Are you . . .??

ADA

(Snorts.)

Hah! Why the fuck would I stick around *here?!*

SAM

Well . . . to help me. . .? With the house, and with Mom's—

ADA

(Slurring a bit.)

Ithink I'vehelped you with *enough*, Sam—thanks.

> SAM *rubs her eyes; keeps drawing. She looks up at* ADA.
>
> *A beat. Then—*

SAM

Can I draw you for a second?

ADA

No.

SAM

But just for a second. . . .

ADA

No, I said!

SAM

But—you're leaving . . . so soon . . . .

ADA

So?

SAM

So I won't get to draw you for . . . so long. . . .

ADA

Euuugh why do you care so much about *drawing me*—that's so *gay*.

Beat. SAM *rubs her eyes.*

SAM

What am I gonna do . . .? Without you here . . .?

ADA

Stop *whining*—it's *party time!*

ADA *dances over to the radio, turns it on. On the radio, Randy Newman sings "You've Got a Friend in Me."*

ADA

(Suddenly cheerful.)

Oh god . . .! This song. . . . Remember this song . . .? Mmmm. . . .

(She sways, dances a little, to the song.)

I always *loved* this song. It's so . . . sweet. . . . So . . . *happy* . . .! So. . . .

(She closes her eyes; sways; sings along to the song a bit:)

You've got a friend in me . . . you've got a friend in me. . . .

(She sways, dances, drunkenly; smiles, woozily.)

I think this might be my most *favorite song* . . .!

A beat. She drains her wine glass. SAM *watches. Then—*

ADA *lunges for the wine bottle—teeters, a bit.*

SAM

Oh! Are you all right . . .? Ada . . .?

ADA *steadies herself by leaning on the table. She lifts her head, heavily; fixes her gaze on* SAM, *blearily.*

ADA

(Slurring, slightly.)

I'm fan*tastic*.

ADA *lifts the wine bottle, tries to pour another glass of wine; has difficulty doing so.* SAM *watches.*

SAM

(With growing concern.)

Ada. . . .

ADA

(Sharp.)

What.

SAM

Are you sure . . . you haven't had . . . enough . . .? To drink . . .?

> *Beat.* ADA *looks at* SAM.

ADA

(Thickly; slurring a bit.)
Areyoufucking *kidding* me.

SAM

No-o. . . .

ADA

(Suddenly tearful.)
My mother just <u>died</u>.

SAM

Ada . . . I *know*. . . .

ADA

(Sloppily; rageful.)
Don't you *EVER* tell me what to do!
> *(Beat.)*
How *DARE* you!
> *(Beat.)*
How*dare*you. . . .

SAM

Okay, Ada—I'm sorry—

ADA

I *deserve* to have fun . . . like everyone else . . .!

> *Beat.* SAM *rubs her eyes.*

SAM

Okay.

ADA

Okay!

SAM

Okay!

> SAM *gets up and turns off the radio. Then—she goes back to her sketchbook.*
>
> ADA *clumsily pours herself a glass of wine; drinks; looks at* SAM.

[handwritten marginal notes:] ada is literall fighting w/t so about the las 4 years wants sam to lay at her feet to get whats owed me to get an addition of guilt to get someo to play by my rules.

A beat. Then—

ADA *grabs the sketchbook out of* SAM*'s hands.*

ADA

Stop *DRAWING* me!

SAM

I'm *n-not . . .!*

ADA

Stop lying! All the *time!*

SAM

I'm—*not*, Ada . . .!

ADA *throws the sketchbook down on the table. Hard.*

ADA

(With a rueful laugh.)
I know. I *know!*

SAM

You know . . . *what* . . . Ada . . .?!

ADA

(Laughs, sloppily.)
You thought you were going to be a "huge success"? Going to the
school *I* wanted to go to?? Hanging out with *my* friend??? Studying
with P.F. *Touchane?!?* I. KNOW. That you never even took one *class*
with him! You didn't have the _guts_! You just stayed in your *dorm room*
and you made *Dorrie* pose for you in _my poses_ with _my beads_ and you
just drew *ME!* Over and over and *over*.
(Beat; gulps wine; laughs.)
What a joke. What a *joke* . . .!

SAM

(Stammering.)
I—I couldn't get into his class . . .! I tried—of course I tried . . .!

ADA *cracks up.*

ADA

(Giggling like a little girl.)
You're lying . . .! You know you lie to yourself, right? Like, *all the
time . . .?!*

SAM

Ada. . . .

ADA

You couldn't take his class 'cause you couldn't draw *anything* that wasn't *me . . .!*

SAM

Ada . . .!

ADA

You wanna draw me sooooo bad. . . .

(*She moves toward* SAM *a bit.*)

You wanna draw this . . .

(*She strikes the modern dance-y pose.*)

You wanna draw *this* . . .

(*She strikes the heroin-chic pose.*)

And oh—OH! You wanna draw *THIS!*

ADA *strikes the sexy pose.*

SAM

Ada! No! I *don't!* <u>Stop!</u>

ADA *begins to rub her breasts, over her shirt, as she walks toward* SAM.

ADA

You want me to stop *this . . .?*

SAM

(*Averting her eyes.*)

Ada, come *on . . .!*

ADA

Oh! You're *shy* now . . .?! You don't wanna draw *this?!?*

She takes one of her breasts out of her shirt. It hangs over the top of her low-cut shirt.

SAM

Ada—I need you, to—

ADA *begins to wrap one of her strands of beads around her breast. She gets up in* SAM*'s face and whispers.*

ADA

You wanna draw it with my *beads* on it . . .?!? C'mon, Sam—draw it. *Draw* it. *DRAW! IT!!!*

SAM *covers her face with her hands; cries.*

ADA *watches; smiles.*

> ADA

HAH.

> *(Beat; she puts her breast away.)*

That's what I thought.

> ADA *grabs the bottle of wine and starts to chug from the bottle.* SAM *watches.*

> SAM

Ada—please . . .! You've had—*enough . . .!*

> ADA *suddenly slams the wine bottle down on the table and charges at* SAM—*brings her face inches away from hers.*

> ADA

> *(Nearly spitting in her face.)*

HEY. I *remember* what happened that night, after Dorrie's graduation party. You thought I wouldn't remember?? 'Cause I was so drunk???

> *(An almost seductive whisper.)*

Well guess what? GUESS WHAT???

> *(A vicious hiss.)*

<u>I remember it like the back of my hand.</u>

> *She looks at* SAM. SAM *looks at her.*

> *A beat. Then—*

> ADA *starts to laugh. She laughs and laughs. She picks up the wine bottle and staggers a few steps backwards— almost falls. Continues to laugh. She drinks wine hungrily from the bottle.*

> *A beat.*

> SAM *rubs her eyes.*

> *A beat.*

> SAM *looks up at her sister. There is a hardness in her eyes we haven't seen before.*

> *A beat. Then—*

> SAM *starts to laugh. She laughs and laughs.*

> SAM

Hahahahaha!

> ADA *stops laughing.*

beat change (handwritten margin note)

ADA

(Thickly.)

What.

SAM

(Laughs even harder.)

Hahahahaha!!!

ADA

What. What?!

SAM

(Still laughing.)

You think *I'm* a joke? 'Cause I never took a class with P.F. *Touchane??* Look at *you . . .!*

(Really looks at ADA; laughs.)

You think you're going to be a "giant *movie star*"?? "Ten feet wide, *twenty feet high*"?!?

(Laughs, darkly.)

I mean, you *know*, right? That that's *never going to happen??* Do you know why???

(Stops laughing.)

Do. You. Know. Why?

(Stares ADA dead in the eyes.)

Because you're *too scared*. You're gonna go to New York and you're just going to drink yourself to *death* in your *dingy* apartment because you are scared *shitless!* And I'm gonna be here finishing my graphic novel and getting *published* and having a *life*, and you'll tell yourself that *I'm* a joke, but you know who the joke is?

(She gets up in ADA's face; a vicious whisper.)

The *alcoholic*. And that's *you*.

> A beat.
>
> They look at each other. Frozen.
>
> Then—
>
> ADA *pours the rest of the wine in the bottle onto* SAM's *sketchbook.*
>
> SAM *looks on, aghast.*

SAM

Ada!

ADA

HAH.

SAM

What the fuck is *wrong with you?!?*

> ADA *tries to drink more wine from the bottle but it is empty.*

ADA

> *(Slamming her hand against the bottom of the bottle, trying to shake any remaining drops into her mouth.)*

Hah. Hah! HAH!

SAM

I fucking *HATE YOU!!!*

> SAM *grabs a dishtowel from a cupboard and begins to mop up her sketchbook.*

> ADA *looks at the ruined sketchbook, giggles.*

ADA

> *(Giggles.)*

Bye bye me . . .!

> ADA *lunges for the sketchbook;* SAM *holds it away, mops at it with the dish towel.*

ADA

Bye bye me me me me ME!

> ADA *tries to grab the sketchbook again.* SAM *pushes her off.*

SAM

STOP IT, ADA! GO AWAY!!!

> *A beat. Then—*

> ADA *pushes* SAM *back. Hard.*

> *A beat. Then—*

> SAM *pushes* ADA *back. Hard.* ADA *staggers back.*

> *A beat. Then—*

> *She pushes* SAM *back. They begin to fight. They wrestle each other. They fight. They fight.*

> *Then—*

> ADA *staggers. Her body suddenly becomes limp. She slumps over.*

SAM

Ada . . .?

> ADA *begins to fall over;* SAM *catches her.*

SAM

Ada . . .!

ADA *melts into* SAM. *Begins to slide down her body.*

SAM *grabs on to* ADA, *hoists her up. Guides her over to a chair at the table. Sits her in it.*

SAM
Here we go. . . . Heeeeeere weeee g-o-o-o-o. . . .

SAM *sits in the chair next to* ADA. *She cradles* ADA *in her arms, and rocks her back and forth.*

ADA *relaxes herself in* SAM*'s arms, seems to almost fall asleep. . . .*

They sit there, ADA*'s head on* SAM*'s bosom, her eyes closed peacefully, and* SAM, *looking down at* ADA. *A Pietà.*

SAM *rubs her eyes with her free hand.*

A beat. Then—

SAM
I'm sorry, Ada.

ADA
(Slurring.)
Ssokay. . . .

SAM
I *love you*, Ada. . . .

ADA
I know. . . .

SAM
I . . .
(Her voice cracking.)
I . . . *need you* . . . Ada. . . .

A beat. Then—

ADA *drunkenly hoists herself up, and grabs the dishtowel off the table. She clumsily ties it around her wrist.*

ADA
(Her eyes barely open.)
Sock-bracelet . . .!

SAM
(Deeply moved.)
Oh!

SAM *can barely catch her breath. She places her hand over her heart. Then—*

She reaches down and pulls her sock off her foot. She tries to tie it around her wrist. It is too short.

SAM
(Her voice almost cracking.)
My sock is too short.

> ADA *reaches under the table and takes her actual sock off. She yanks herself up, and clumsily ties her sock onto* SAM*'s wrist.*

ADA
(Grinning like a fool; slurring her words.)
Sock-braceletsisters. . . .

SAM
(Tears in her eyes.)
Sock-bracelet sisters . . .!

> *They make their sock-bracelets play with each other and kiss each other, etc.*

ADA & SAM
(Together; improvising a song.)
Sock-bracelet sisters, la la la la la la, singing in the la la, loodie doodie doo doo. . . .

> *They crack each other up with their made-up lyrics.*

ADA & SAM
Hahahahaha!

> *They make their sock-bracelets high-five each other.*

ADA & SAM
(High-fiving.)
Yeah!

> *They crack up.*

ADA & SAM
Hahahahaha!!

> *When the laughter dies down—*

> ADA *suddenly lunges toward* SAM *and grabs her hand; she claps* SAM*'s hand over her mouth.*

> *A beat. Then—*

> SAM *removes it, slowly. Then—*

> ADA, *bleary-eyed, licks it, slowly.*

> *They look at each other. Then—*

ADA *playfully swats* SAM *in the face with her sock-bracelet arm.*

                          ADA
          (Playfully swatting.)
Bam!

                          SAM
          (Falling back with glee.)
Ohh!
          They laugh.

                    ADA & SAM
Hahahahaha!!!
          *They stand up and proceed to play-fight—*SAM *shoves* ADA
          back, playfully.

                          SAM
          (Playfully shoving.)
BOOM!!

                          ADA
OOOH!!
          They laugh.

                    ADA & SAM
HAHAHAHAHAHAHAHA!!!
          *Then—*ADA *shoves* SAM, *hard, back.*

                          ADA
          (Mirthfully shoving.)
SHAZZZAAAMMMMMMMMMM!!!!!!

                          SAM
Whoa!
          SAM *falls backwards, through the open cellar door . . .*

          . . . and down the stairs.

          ADA *gasps.*

          She watches, silent.

          We hear SAM *fall all the way down the stairs.*

          A long, terrible silence.

          Then—
                          ADA
          (Tiny voice.)
Sam . . .?

SCENE 12

The voices of three girls scream: **"ADULTHOOD!!!"**

A long, long blackout.

We begin to hear ADA *talking, softly. We can hear the muffled sounds of city life outside.*

Lights creep up, painfully slowly, on ADA. *She sits in a tiny pool of light, on the floor of her apartment in New York City. A hand mirror is on the floor in front of her. She drinks wine from the bottle. A cigarette burns in a nearby ashtray.*

Her speech is slurred. Her eyes are half-shut, and swollen. She is very, very drunk.

Throughout this monologue, she empties a bag of cocaine onto the hand mirror and cuts it up with a credit card.

ADA

I just . . . can't help but . . . think I am . . . ex*tremely* beautiful. . . .

(She cuts up the cocaine.)

Sometimes . . .? I'll look at my face in the mirror, and I'll see . . . me. . . .

(She gulps some wine, hungrily.)

And I'm always. . . so pleasantly surprised. . . .

(She puts the wine glass down, too hard; attempts to strike her heroin-chic pose.)

Because I'm . . . *gorgeous*. . . .

(A beat; she rubs some cocaine on her gums.)

. . . Everyone always said I shiiiiiine like a star . . .! And it's still true. If a tree falls in the . . . even if there aren't any other trees around, I'm still. . . . you know???

(She drains her wine glass.)

Eaaaat shit, eat shit all day, and wipe it off your face, like the . . . and no one knows it. . . .

(She clumsily pours the dregs of the wine bottle into her wine glass.)

But you can *see* that—other people can *see* that. . . . They don't wanna *admit* that 'cause they're. . . . When people wanna *be* you, you have to <u>watch your back</u>!

(She slams the little bit of wine in her glass down her throat.)

You can't trust *anyone*. You have to <u>get away</u>. . . .

(She smiles.)

And that's what I did . . .!

(She takes a drag off her cigarette.)

But *I* know what's coming for me. If you don't see it, then I feel sorry for you. 'Cause when I'm . . . you're gonna . . . ohhhh!

(She starts to laugh. . .)

Oh!

(She laughs and laughs.)

Oh ho ho ho ho! You're gonna—and then I'll be . . .! And who'll . . .?! Oh, no. No no.

She laughs and laughs and laughs, woozily, bleary-eyed. She starts to cry. She laughs and cries.

ADA

What a joke . . .! What a joke . . .

She almost nods off. . . .

A beat. Then—

She jerks her head up. She pulls a rolled-up dollar bill out of her bra, puts it on the hand mirror, leans down and snorts a line of coke. She snorts another line. She looks up. Her eyes are red and wet.

ADA

(A whisper.)

You said I was scared? Well guess what. Can you guess?

(She waits.)

Can you?

(She listens.)

Oh you can't? Well GUESS WHAT?

(A vicious hiss.)

<u>*I don't care enough to be scared.*</u>

> *She giggles, girlishly—almost flirtatiously. She leans down and snorts another line of coke.*

ADA

(A whisper.)

I don't even care . . .!

> *(She rubs more coke on her gums; giggles, impishly.)*

I . . . *don't* . . . *care* . . .! About a darrrrrrnnnn thinnnnnggg. . . .

> *(She begins to nod off . . . she slurs . . .)*

Idon'tevencare. . . .

> *She falls asleep, sitting up.*

SCENE 13

The kitchen in the sisters' childhood home. SAM *sits in a wheelchair.* DORRIE *sits opposite* SAM *in a chair.*

They play the same hand game they played in college, only now it is painfully slow and labored.

After a certain point, they just let their hands fall into their laps.

A beat.

Then—

SAM

God, I hate it here.

DORRIE

I know what you mean.

SAM

You're just saying that 'cause I said it.

DORRIE

Yeah.

> *Beat. Then—*
>
> SAM *starts to laugh.*

SAM

Hah! You know? I really thought we would never speak again. After I popped that balloon, in your ear? I thought that would be the last time I'd ever even *speak* to you . . .!

> *(Beat.)*

And now you *live* with me . . .!

> *(Laughs, darkly.)*

Hah. What a *joke.* . . .

> *A beat.*

DORRIE

> *(Softly.)*

She's doing the best she can, Sam.

> SAM *glares at* DORRIE.

A beat. Then—

SAM

I don't care anymore. I. Don't. Care.

She starts to wheel away.

DORRIE

Wait!

SAM

What?

Beat.

DORRIE

Do you want me to . . . brush . . . your hair . . .?

Beat.

SAM

Fine.

DORRIE *beams; she gets the hairbrush out of the drawer, crosses behind* SAM *and begins to brush her hair.*

Some quiet moments of just brushing. DORRIE *hums quietly to herself.*

DORRIE *finishes brushing* SAM*'s hair. Pats her freshly-brushed hair.*

DORRIE

There.

SAM

(Patting her hair.)

Thank you, Dorrie.

DORRIE

(With a terribly sweet smile.)

Thank *you*, Sam.

Suddenly, SAM *reaches out her arms to* DORRIE, *for a hug.*

SAM

(On the verge of tears.)

Dorrie . . .!

DORRIE *lunges in and hugs* SAM, *tightly.*

DORRIE

Oh, Sammy . . .!

(Beat.)

She'll come back.

(Beat.)

I *know* she will.

SAM

(Sobbing into DORRIE*'s torso.)*

I didn't *know* . . .! If I *knew?* If I knew it would . . . turn *out*—like this . . .?! I never would have—!

She can't finish.

She just sobs and sobs, into DORRIE*'s bosom.*

DORRIE *strokes her hair, her heart breaking for her friend.*

DORRIE

Shhh . . . shhh. . . .

SAM *sobs and sobs into* DORRIE*'s bosom;* DORRIE *lets her, strokes her.*

A beat. Then—

DORRIE

(Getting an idea.)

Oh—I have a good idea . . .!

(Pulling away; excited.)

Why don't I go get your sketchbook, Sam?

DORRIE *strikes the sexy pose.*

SAM *looks at* DORRIE *in horror; pulls away. Her eyes harden.*

SAM

What are you—*mocking* me?! You *know* I can't draw without her here . . .!

(Snorts.)

What a joke . . .! I thought I was going to go to *college*, and study with P.F. *Touchane*, and publish my graphic *novel*, and. . . .

(She laughs and cries.)

What a joke. . . . What a miserable, miserable joke . . .!

She cries. DORRIE *tries to hug her.*

SAM

(Swatting DORRIE *away.)*

Enough, Dorrie! Leave me alone.

DORRIE

You need a hug. . . .

SAM

Eugggh why do you care so much about *hugging?* That's so *gay.*

DORRIE *tries to hug her again.*

SAM

Get *away* from me Dorrie—I *told* you!

SAM *shoves* DORRIE *off her, violently.* DORRIE *slams into the wall. She starts to cry.*

DORRIE

You *need* me. Sam. . . .

SAM

(A vicious hiss.)

I don't need *anything*—except what I can't *have. . .!*

DORRIE

(Tearful.)

What do you want, Sam??? You can *tell* me . . .! Dorrie won't judge you. Dorrie will only *love* you. Dorrie will only *listen . . .!*

DORRIE *tries to hug* SAM *again. This time,* SAM *wraps her fingers around* DORRIE *'s neck and squeezes.*

DORRIE *gasps.*

SAM *squeezes.*

DORRIE *'s face gets very red.*

A beat.

SAM *'s fingers quiver. Her mouth hardens into a line.*

A beat.

DORRIE *'s face turns purple.*

A beat.

DORRIE *'s eyes roll into the back of her head.*

A beat. Then—

SAM *lets go.*

DORRIE *falls to the floor.*

She heaves.

She heaves.

A beat. Then—

DORRIE *scampers to the corner of the room, like a beaten animal. She trembles. She shakes.*

SAM *doesn't look at her.*

A beat. Then—

> DORRIE
> *(Trembling, crying.)*

You don't . . . *like* me . . . very much . . . Sam. . . .

> SAM
> *(Not looking at* DORRIE.*)*

Well, you're not a very likable *person*, are you, Dorrie?

Beat. DORRIE *whimpers and shakes.*

> SAM
> *(Finally looking at* DORRIE.*)*

Uggggh, it was a *joke!* You don't have a very good sense of humor.

Beat. DORRIE *whimpers and shakes.*

> SAM
> *(Beckoning* DORRIE.*)*

Come here, Dorrie. Give Sammy a hug.

> DORRIE
> *(Shaking, terrified.)*

I think . . .

> SAM

You think *what*, Dorrie?!

> DORRIE
> *(With tremendous reluctance.)*

I think . . . I should . . . maybe . . . *go* . . . Sam. . . .

Beat.

> SAM

Go???

> DORRIE
> *(Crying.)*

Sam . . .!

> SAM

You can't—*leave* me, Dorrie . . .!

> DORRIE

I don't know what to *do*, Sam . . .!

SAM *look at* DORRIE, *incredulous.*

A beat. Then—

> SAM

I'm sorry, Dorrie . . .!

> DORRIE
> *(Rubbing her throat; reticent.)*

Okay. . . .

> SAM

I love you, Dorrie. . . .!

> DORRIE
> *(Still rubbing her wound; still reticent.)*

I know. . . .

> SAM

I . . .

> *(Her voice cracking, ever so slightly.)*

I . . . *need you* . . . Dorrie. . . .

> *Beat.*

> DORRIE

Y-you—do???

A beat. SAM *nods, slowly.*

She looks at DORRIE *with ferocious intensity. Wipes her tears away.*

> SAM

Ada's dead to me, Dorrie.

> *(Beat.)*

You're my Ada, now.

A beat. Then—

> DORRIE
> *(A sudden light in her eyes.)*

I'm up at bat . . .!

A beat. SAM *smiles.*

> SAM
> *(A new light in her eyes, too.)*

You really are this time.

SCENE 14

A flashback.

The kitchen in the girls' childhood home. SAM *(not in a wheelchair) helps a stumbling* ADA *into the kitchen, from outside. It is right after* DORRIE*'s high school graduation party. It is dark outside.* ADA *is wasted.*

> SAM
> *(Very gently.)*

Here we go. . . . Heeeeeere weeee g-o-o-o-o. . . .

> ADA
> *(Slurring.)*

ThankyouSam. . . . Thankyou. . . .

> SAM *helps* ADA *into a chair.*

> ADA *slumps into the chair; she looks like a rag doll, trying to sit herself up.*

> SAM
> *(Giggles a bit.)*

Wow—I don't know how you got so *drunk . . .!*

> ADA *slumps over.*

> SAM
> *(Laughs.)*

Lemme get you some water.

> ADA

I need more.

> SAM
> *(Laughing.)*

What?

> ADA

I need more.
> *(Beat.)*

Alcohol.

> *A beat.* SAM *looks at* ADA *with a bit of concern.*

SAM

Ada. . . .

ADA

What.

SAM

You're already . . . really . . . drunk. . . .

> ADA *lifts her heavy head up—she stares* SAM *down.*

ADA

(In a voice of pure need and urgency.)

<u>Give it to me.</u>

> *A beat.* SAM *is taken aback.*

SAM

Fine. Just. . . . Wow.

> SAM *finds the whiskey bottle and a glass; pours some whiskey into the glass. Then, she opens the refrigerator and takes out a glass bottle of milk. She fills the rest of the glass with milk, slides it over to* ADA.

SAM

(Sardonically.)

Here you go—your new favorite.

ADA

Feedittome.

SAM

What?

ADA

(Suddenly playful.)

FEEDittome!

SAM

(Laughing; uncomfortable.)

Oh my gosh! This is funny—okay. . . .

> *She clumsily tries to feed* ADA *the drink. It sort of works.*
>
> *After a few sips,* ADA *slumps her head down.* SAM *puts the drink down on the table.*
>
> *A beat.* ADA *sits, slumped.* SAM *looks at her with love.*
>
> *A beat. Then—*
>
> ADA *suddenly jerks her head up, looks at* SAM.

ADA

Gimmeakiss.

SAM

What?

ADA

(Sweetly, flirty, funny.)
GimmeaKISS!!!

SAM

A—a *kiss . . .?*

ADA

(Making kissy faces at SAM.*)*
Mwah mwah *mwah . . .!*

SAM

(Laughing uncomfortably.)
I'm not gonna kiss—

> *Before* SAM *can finish,* ADA *lunges forward and plants a big kiss on* SAM*'s lips. Then she pulls away, slumps back to her sitting position in her chair.*

ADA

(Nodding clumsily again.)
Hee hee.

SAM

(Frozen; eyes fixed on ADA.*)*
You're—you're ridiculous.

> ADA *slumps down onto* SAM*'s shoulder, relaxes herself into* SAM*'s bosom.*

> *They sit there,* ADA*'s head on* SAM*'s bosom, her eyes closed peacefully, and* SAM, *looking down at* ADA. *A Pietà.*

> SAM *rubs her eyes with her free hand.*

> *A beat. Then—*

ADA

Ahneedagotobed.

> *Beat.*

SAM

(Rubbing her eyes.)
That's a good idea. Let's go to bed. Come on.

> SAM *stands up, and hoists* ADA *up, with much effort.* ADA *has a hard time standing up; once up, she weaves back and forth.*

She places her hands on ADA*'s shoulders to steady her.*

SAM

Here we go. . . . Heeeere weeee go-o-o-o. . . .

It works; she has steadied her.

*They stand, facing each other—*ADA*, bleary-eyed, staring at* SAM*, and* SAM*, clear-eyed, looking at* ADA*.*

A beat. Then—

ADA

Ahloveyou.

Beat.

SAM

(Struck.)

You never say that to me. . . .

ADA

Butahmeanit.

SAM *rubs her eyes. A beat. Then—*

SAM

(Tears brimming.)

I love you too, Ada.

SAM *reaches out and strokes* ADA*'s hair.* ADA *smiles, and lets her.*

*A beat. Then—*SAM *leans in, and gently, very gently, kisses* ADA *on the lips.*

The kiss is long.

It lasts.

It lasts.

Then—

ADA *pulls away.*

Her face stays close to SAM*'s.*

A beat. Then—

ADA

Thankyou.

Beat.

SAM

Thank *you*, Ada.

They look at each other.

SCENE 15

SAM *and* DORRIE *in the kitchen of the sisters' childhood home.* SAM *sits in her wheelchair.*

They are older now—in their late twenties, probably. They look better—healthier. They wear bright-ish colors. There is some color in their cheeks.

They play their hand game. Now, they play with vigor and— amazingly—some joy, seemingly. They smile. They laugh.

                    SAM
Oh!

                    DORRIE
Oh!

                    SAM
We're going so fast!

                    DORRIE
We're going *so . . .! FAST . . .!*

                    SAM
I don't think we've ever gone this *fast*, before . . .!

                    DORRIE
I don't think we have, *either . . .!*

                    SAM
        (Totally gleeful.)
We're *winning at life . . .!*

                    DORRIE
        (Totally gleeful, also.)
We totally *are . . .!*

        Suddenly, DORRIE *messes up.*

                    SAM
You messed up, that was sixty-three.

                    DORRIE
I know—I'm sorry, I thought it was sixty-two.
        A beat. Then—

                            SAM
        (Shrugs.)
It's okay—my hands were getting tired, anyway.

                            DORRIE
        (Smiles.)
Me too.

        SAM *smiles at* DORRIE.

        A beat. Then—

        SAM *reaches her hand out to* DORRIE*, and clasps* DORRIE*'s
        hand.*

                            SAM
You're my buddy, Dorrie.

                            DORRIE
        (With deep gratitude.)
Oh, Sam. . . .

                            SAM
You're my lil' pal.

                            DORRIE
        (Beams.)
You don't know how happy you make me.

        They hold hands.

        A beat. Then—

                            SAM
Can you pour me a glass of milk? I'd do it myself but I'm paralyzed
from the waist down.

        They giggle.

                    SAM & DORRIE
Hehehehehe!

                            DORRIE
        (Getting up.)
Nothing would give me greater pleasure.

        Suddenly, through the door—

        ADA *stumbles in.*

        *Her face is white. She has dark, dark circles under her
        eyes. She looks gaunt, strung-out, exhausted—nearly dead.*

        She clutches her arm in a strange way.

        ADA *looks at* SAM.

A beat.

SAM *looks at* ADA.

A beat.

DORRIE *looks at* ADA *and* SAM.

A beat. Then—

SAM *breaks her gaze with* ADA, *and wheels away.*

She wheels into the other room.

ADA *is left alone with* DORRIE.

DORRIE

(Very gently.)

Hi, Ada. . . .

ADA *crumbles.*

ADA

(Crying.)

Oh Dorrie . . .!

DORRIE

Ada. . . .

ADA

(Hysterical.)

I didn't know—I didn't *know* . . .!

Beat.

DORRIE

I know.

ADA

(Desperate.)

Please, Dorrie!

DORRIE

What . . .?

ADA

Help me . . .!

She sobs and sobs. DORRIE *watches her, at a loss.*

A beat. Then—

DORRIE *approaches* ADA. *She slowly puts her arms around her. She hugs her.* ADA *lets herself be hugged—probably for the first time in many, many years.*

She guides her over to a chair at the table. Sits her in it.

DORRIE

(Guiding ADA *into a chair.)*

Here we go. . . . Heeeeeere weeee g-o-o-o-o. . . .

ADA *weeps and weeps into* DORRIE*'s bosom.* DORRIE *rocks
her.*

ADA

(Crying.)

. . . it feels so good when you hold me, Dorrie . . . just like this. . . .

DORRIE

(Rocking her.)

Mmmm. . . .

ADA

Oh, Dorrie. . . . I can't . . . *do it* . . . anymore . . .!

DORRIE

Ohhh, Ada. . . .

ADA

I can't keep . . . *living* . . . like this . . .!

A beat. DORRIE *considers.* . . .

DORRIE

(Stroking ADA*'s hair.)*

(Beat.)

We'll *help* you, Ada. You just have to . . .

(Beat; she considers . . .)

. . . I think you just have to . . . say you're sorry. . . . I'll go get Sam, and
you'll say you're sorry, and everything will be all *right . . .!* You'll get better, Ada—you'll be a new person . . .! Like you were never sad, or sick,
or scared, or—or *anything* bad. . . . You'll be *clean*, Ada.

(She beams.)

We all will . . .!

A beat. ADA *crumbles.*

ADA

Will she ever get out of that *wheelchair . . .?!*

A beat. DORRIE *looks at* ADA*, confused.*

DORRIE

No, Ada. . . .

ADA

I thought I'd come home, and . . . she'd be *walking . . .!*

                              DORRIE

(Very sad.)

That doesn't make any *sense*, Ada. . . .

> *A beat.* ADA*'s eyes fix with a steely resolve.*

                              ADA

Go get her.

> *A beat.* DORRIE*'s eyes open wide.*

                              DORRIE

(With glee.)

Oh, Ada . . .!

> DORRIE *runs into the other room.*
>
> ADA *quickly goes over to the sink and rolls up the left sleeve of her shirt, revealing several paper towels soaked through in blood. She peels the paper towels off her arm and throws them in the trash. She winces at the pain. She rips a few paper towels off a roll on the counter and lays them on her arm. She rolls her sleeve back down. Then—*
>
> SAM *wheels in.*
>
> ADA *turns.*
>
> *She looks at her sister.*
>
> *They look at each other.*
>
> *They don't say anything.*
>
> *A beat. Then—*

                              SAM

What . . . *happened* . . . to you . . .?

> ADA *cries.*

                              ADA

You were *right* . . .!

> *(Cries.)*

I was too scared. I was scared *shitless*, Sam. You were <u>*right.*</u>

> *(Beat; she weeps.)*

I don't want to . . . be . . . an *adult* . . .! Anymore. . . .

> *(Beat; she weeps.)*

I want to . . . be . . . a *kid* . . . again . . .!

Beat. She cries, pathetically.

SAM

I don't care, Ada.

ADA

(Hysterical.)

I want to *die*, Sam . . .!

Beat.

SAM

(Snorts.)

Why don't you just have a drink?

ADA *cries.*

ADA

I can't . . .!

(She weeps.)

I can't *ever drink again . . .!*

SAM *laughs, darkly.*

ADA *looks on, at a loss. Then—*

ADA *lifts her sleeve, removes the bloody paper towels from her arm and shows* SAM *her fresh wounds.*

SAM *looks at* ADA *with utter revulsion. A beat; then—*

SAM

I still don't care.

SAM *starts to wheel away from* ADA.

A beat. Then—

ADA

(Softly.)

I'm sorry, Sam.

SAM

(Reticent.)

Okay. . . .

ADA

I love you, Sam.

SAM

(With tremendous reticence.)

I know. . . .

ADA

I . . .

(Her voice cracking, ever so slightly.)

I . . . *need you* . . . Sam. . . .

Beat.

SAM

You've never—*said* that . . . to me. . . .

ADA

But I mean it.

A beat. SAM *rubs her eyes.*

SAM

(Tears brimming.)

Thank you, Ada.

ADA

Thank *you*, Sam.

A beat. Then—

SAM *turns to look at* ADA.

They look at each other.

A beat. Then—

Huge smiles emerge on their faces. They beam at each other.

A beat. Then—

DORRIE *comes running back in.*

DORRIE

(On pins and needles.)

Did you guys make up?!?

The sisters look at each other.

SAM

(Smiling.)

Yes.

ADA

(Smiling.)

Yes!

ADA & SAM

Yes!

DORRIE

OHHHHHHH YAAAAAAAAYYYYYYY!!!!!!!!!!!!!

> DORRIE *runs over to* SAM *and hugs her, fiercely. Then, she runs over to* ADA *and hugs her, fiercely.*

DORRIE

This is the *BEST DAY OF MY LIFE!!!!!!!!!!!!!!!*

> *They all three crack up.*

SAM & DORRIE & ADA

HAHAHAHAHAHAHAHA!!!

> *Then—*DORRIE *runs over to* SAM *and sits on her lap.*

DORRIE

Oh, Sammy—*Sam . . .!* This is what we've been *waiting* for . . .! All these years—all these *years . . .!*

SAM

> *(Beams.)*

I know. I *know . . .!*

DORRIE

Ada! Come here!!

> ADA *comes over.*

DORRIE

Sit!!!

> DORRIE *pats her lap.* ADA *laughs, and sits on* DORRIE, *who is sitting on top of* SAM.

> *All three girls sit on top of each other, in* SAM*'s wheelchair.*

> *They let out a simultaneous, satisfied sigh.*

SAM & ADA & DORRIE

> *(A simultaneous sigh.)*

Huuuuuuuuuuuuhhhhhhhhhh. . . .

> *A beat. Then—*

DORRIE

Hey guys?

ADA & SAM

Yeah?

DORRIE

This is going to be the best sleepover ever!

ADA & SAM

Yeah!

SAM

(So excited.)

We can stay up late and watch horror movies and—

DORRIE

(Cutting SAM *off, with an amazing idea')*

Oh, and *Sam!* Maybe you could even—maybe you could . . . *draw* . . . Ada . . .!

SAM

Oh . . .!

SAM *looks at* ADA. *Tears of joy fill her eyes.*

SAM

I still have my sketchbook—I haven't used it in years but . . . I know *right* where it is . . .!

DORRIE

I'LL GO GET IT RIGHT NOW!!!

SAM

Oh, *thank* you, Dorrie!

DORRIE

Nothing would give me greater pleasure. . .!

DORRIE *hoists* ADA *off her, and begins to hurry off; then, she stops, and turns back to them—*

DORRIE

Oh, I'm so . . . *happy* . . .! This is how I always *wanted* it to end!

(Beat; she looks at them, drinks them in with her eyes.)

Sam and Ada and Dorrie. All together. Under one roof. Forever. And ever. And ever.

(Beat; she looks at them, overcome with joy.)

I love you both, so much.

She hurries off.

ADA *stays standing, looks in the direction in which* DORRIE *just left.*

Her eyes suddenly seem far away. . . .

*Then—*ADA *crosses to the shelves, which are still lined with all the alcohol bottles. She examines them.*

She zeroes in on the shining blue bottle of gin.

SAM *watches* ADA.

A beat. Then—

SAM

What's *wrong*, Ada . . .?

ADA

(Distracted.)
What? Nothing.

SAM

You seem weird now.

ADA *turns and looks at* SAM.

ADA

Does she sleep in my bed?

Beat.

SAM

Ada. . . .

ADA

Does she brush your hair??

SAM

Ada, please. . . .

ADA

Does she pose for your drawings, still???

Beat.

SAM

Ada, come on. She's all I had.

ADA *turns away, looks at the blue bottle.* SAM *watches, with alarm.*

SAM

Ada. . . .

A beat. Then—

SAM *begins to roll up the left sleeve of her sweater.*

SAM

Look.

ADA *turns and looks.* SAM *holds out her arm, which is riddled with scars—scars that look almost exactly like the fresh wounds on* ADA*'s arm.*

ADA

Oh!

SAM

Shhh . . .! Dorrie doesn't know. . . .

> ADA *approaches* SAM *and gently touches her sister's arm.*

ADA

When did you . . . *do* . . . this . . .?

SAM

A while ago.

ADA

Why . . .?

SAM

> *(With a sad smile.)*

Because of you.

> *(Beat.)*

Why did *you?*

ADA

> *(With a sad smile, also.)*

Because of *you.*

SAM

> *(Deeply moved.)*

Oh . . .!

> ADA *sits in* SAM*'s lap. They make their matching arm-wrist wounds play with each other and kiss each other, etc.*

ADA & SAM

> *(Singing.)*

Sock-bracelet sisters, la la la la la la, singing in the la la, loodie doodie doo doo. . . .

> *They crack each other up with their made-up lyrics.*

ADA & SAM

Hahahahaha!

> *They make their wounds high-five each other.*

ADA & SAM

Yeah!

ADA

> *(Pulling away, grabbing her wounded arm.)*

Ow!

SAM

Oh!

Beat. Then—

They crack up.

ADA & SAM

HAHAHAHAHAHAHAHAHAHA!!!

When the laughter dies down. . . .

They let out a simultaneous, contented sigh.

ADA & SAM

(A simultaneous sigh.)

Huuuuuuuuuuuhhhhhhhhhh. . . .

Beat. Then—

ADA

(Smiling at her sister.)

I'm glad it's not weird anymore.

SAM

(Smiling at her sister.)

Me too.

They look at each other; smile.

They pull their sleeves back down over their wounds.

A beat. Then—

ADA

(Smiling.)

Go tell her.

Beat.

SAM

(Confused.)

. . . what . . .?

ADA

(Sweetly.)

Tell her to leave. You don't need her anymore. You have me, now.

SAM

But—

ADA

(Suddenly venomous.)

But *what?!*

Beat. SAM*'s eyes fill with tears.*

> SAM

I *love* her, Ada . . .!

> ADA

(Snorts.)

You don't *love* her, Sam! She's *Dorrie*, Sam! She's just a big dummy—a big old *fool* . . .! Who needs *Dorrie*?! When you *have me.* You *HAVE ME*.

(Beat.)

But only if she's gone.

> SAM*'s chin trembles. She looks at* ADA *with tear-filled eyes.*

> SAM

(With utter desperation.)

Ada . . . please . . .!

> ADA *looks at* SAM*, twirls a strand of* SAM*'s hair around her finger.*

> *A beat. Then—*

> *Slowly, very slowly,* ADA *leans in and kisses* SAM*, very softly, on the lips.*

> *A beat.*

> ADA *pulls back.*

> *She stays on* SAM*'s lap.* SAM *looks at her, enraptured. . . .*

> *A beat. Then—*

> SAM*'s eyes fix with a steely resolve.*

> SAM

Dorrie . . .!

> ADA *smiles, and gets off* SAM*'s lap.*

> DORRIE

(OS.)

Coming, Sammy . . .!

> *A beat. Then—*

> DORRIE *comes running in, carrying* SAM*'s sketchbook.*

> ADA *sits in a chair at the kitchen table and watches the interaction.*

DORRIE

I found your sketchbook, Sam! I wiped all the dust off, and it's—good
as . . .

> (Notices the somber air in the room.)

. . . new. . . .

SAM

> (Hoarsely.)

Come here, Dorrie. . . .

> Beat. DORRIE comes over to SAM.

DORRIE

What's *wrong*, Sam . . .?

> SAM points toward ADA.

SAM

> (Pointing.)

Look what you did to her, Dorrie. *Look what you did.*

DORRIE

I didn't . . . do *anything* . . .! Sam. . . .

SAM

> (Hoarsely.)

I need you to leave. I don't need you anymore. I have Ada, now.

DORRIE

But—

SAM

But *what?!*

DORRIE

You—love me, Sam . . .!

> SAM rubs her eyes.

SAM

> (Trying not to cry).

I don't *love* you, Dorrie! You're *Dorrie, Dorrie!* You're just a big dummy
—a big old *fool* . . .! Who needs *Dorrie!?* When I *have Ada.* I *HAVE
ADA.*

> (Beat; hoarsely.)

But only if you're gone.

DORRIE

> (Weeping hysterically.)

You can have us *both*, Sam . . .!

> SAM shakes her head, darkly.

SAM

(Beginning to cry.)
I have to choose . . .!

DORRIE

Don't—*do* this . . .! Sam!

DORRIE *tries to hug* SAM.

SAM

(Pushing DORRIE *away.)*
Go *away*, Dorrie!

DORRIE *tries to hug* SAM, *again.*

DORRIE

(Clawing at SAM.)
You *need* me, Sam . . .!

SAM

(Shoving DORRIE *away.)*
I *don't* need you, Dorrie—I *don't! I don't!*

DORRIE
(Hysterical; uncomprehending.)
What are you *doing* . . .?! Dorrie will only *love* you!! Dorrie will only
listen!!!

DORRIE *frantically tries to hug* SAM *again. This time,* SAM
wraps her fingers around DORRIE *'s neck and squeezes.*

DORRIE *gasps.*

SAM *squeezes.*

DORRIE *'s face gets very red.*

A beat.

SAM *'s fingers quiver. Her mouth hardens into a line.*

A beat.

DORRIE *'s face turns purple.*

A beat.

DORRIE *'s eyes roll into the back of her head.*

A beat. Then—

SAM *lets go.*

DORRIE *falls to the floor.*

A beat.

She lies there. She lies there. Not moving. Not breathing. Her face turns white.

She is dead.

SAM *looks at* DORRIE*'s dead body; she pants; she shakes.*

ADA *looks on; smiles a little smile. Then—she gets up and walks over to the shelves of alcohol bottles. She examines the blue bottle of gin. She gets on her tiptoes and takes the blue bottle off the shelf. She turns it around in her hands, looks at it.*

A beat. Then—

SAM
(Eyes glassy; with the voice of a little girl.)
I did it, Ada. . . .

ADA
Good girl, Sam.

ADA *unscrews the cap of the blue bottle, and . . . begins to pour the bottle down the kitchen sink.*

SAM *turns, and looks.*

SAM
(Re: the bottles.)
What are you—

ADA
(Cutting her off.)
It's better this way.

ADA *continues to pour.* SAM *watches.*

A beat. Then—

SAM
Can I draw you for a second?

ADA *watches the last of the gin go down the drain.*

ADA
Mm-hmmmmmmm!

SAM
Will you hand me my sketchbook? I'd do it myself, but I'm paralyzed from the waist down.

They laugh.

ADA & SAM

Hahahahaha!

ADA bends down near DORRIE *'s dead body and picks up* SAM *'s sketchbook.*

ADA

(Handing the sketchbook to SAM*.)*

Here ya go!

SAM

(Taking the sketchbook.)

Thanks! Do you wanna put on some music?

ADA

Yuppers!

ADA steps over DORRIE *'s dead body to get to the radio. Turns it on. Flips through the stations.*

As she does so, SAM *reaches into a cupboard and finds a bottle of whiskey. She unscrews the cap. She wheels over to the refrigerator, opens it. Takes out a glass bottle of milk.*

ADA turns the radio to a station that is playing Randy Newman's "You've Got a Friend in Me."

ADA

(Chuckling to herself.)

Oh god . . .! This song. . . . Remember this song . . .? Mmmm. . . .

She turns and sees that SAM *is holding the bottle of milk in one hand. . . and the bottle of whiskey in the other.*

A beat.

ADA

Oh.

SAM

(Chipperly.)

Could you grab us some glasses? From up there???

(Nods toward the kitchen cabinets.)

I'd do it myself, but I'm paralyzed from the waist down.

(She laughs.)

Hahahahaha!

A beat. ADA *swallows.*

SAM

You didn't think that was funny . . .?

ADA

Sam. . . .

SAM

(Innocently.)

. . . what . . .??

ADA

(Almost trembling in fear.)

I—I c-can't. . . .

SAM

Come on, Ada—we deserve to have fun, like everyone else . . .!

ADA *bites her lip, holds back tears. Then—*

She reaches up toward the kitchen cabinet, opens it, takes out two glasses. Tremblingly, she hands them to SAM.

SAM

Thanks! And do you mind. . .

SAM *holds out the bottle of whiskey to* ADA.

Eyes glassy and transfixed on the whiskey, ADA *takes the bottle from* SAM. SAM *pops the top off the milk bottle, and pours some milk into each glass, filling each one halfway.*

SAM

Mmmmm. . . .

ADA *stares at the whiskey bottle in her hand.*

SAM

Can you pour . . .?

Almost as if in a daze, ADA *unscrews the top off the whiskey bottle, and pours some whiskey into each glass.*

When she's finished pouring . . .

SAM

(Handing a glass to ADA.*)*

Here ya go!

*Eyes glassy and wide—and completely transfixed on the glass—*ADA *takes the glass from* SAM.

SAM *watches, rapt—a faint, faint smile creeping across her lips.*

SAM

Cheers!

As if in a trance, ADA *brings the glass over to the table. She places it down on the table. She sits in a chair, her eyes never leaving the glass.*

SAM *watches, rapt.*

A beat. Then—

SAM *begins to sketch* ADA. *She sings along to the radio as she sketches.*

SAM

You've got a friend in me . . .

ADA *looks at the glass.*

SAM

You've got a friend in me . . .

ADA *looks at the glass.*

A beat.

She looks.

A beat.

Then—

She drinks.

She drinks. She nearly drains the whole glass.

SAM *watches the whole thing. Sketches. Smiles. Sings.*

SAM

You've got troubles, well I've got 'em too . . .

ADA *fishes in her bag and finds a cigarette.*

SAM

There isn't anything I wouldn't do for you . . .

ADA *lights the cigarette. She inhales. Her eyes fill with tears.*

SAM

(Cheerfully.)

Can you open the cellar door? If you're gonna smoke?

> ADA *takes a huge sip of whiskey. Then, glass in one hand, cigarette in the other, she rises and crosses to the cellar door. She opens it. She looks.*
>
> SAM *continues to sketch* ADA. *She sings to herself as she sketches.*

SAM

(Singing.)

We stick together and we see it through . . .
Oh, you've got a friend in me . . .
You've got a friend in me . . .
You've got a friend in me . . .!

> ADA *looks down at the staircase.*
>
> *She drinks. She cries.*
>
> SAM *sketches, looks up at* ADA.

SAM

(With a smile.)

You've always been soooooo pretty, Ada. . . .

> *Randy Newman's "You've Got a Friend in Me" swells, as lights fade.*
>
> *Blackout.*

END OF PLAY

ALSO BY HALLEY FEIFFER AND AVAILABLE FROM THE OVERLOOK PRESS

Ella is a precocious and fiercely competitive actress whose aims in life are making her famous playwright father David proud—and becoming famous herself. Over the course of a boozy, drug-fueled evening, Ella and David deliberate over whether to read the reviews of her off-Broadway debut . . . and things unravel from there.

"Bone-chilling."　　　**—Charles Isherwood, *The New York Times***

"Viciously funny and brutally effective. Feiffer takes a tough look at the forces that can bring us to our knees."　　　**—Adam Feldman, *Time Out New York***

$14.95　978-1-4683-1108-2

THE OVERLOOK PRESS　•　NEW YORK　•　WWW.OVERLOOKPRESS.COM